Keeping Ex-Offenders Free!

Pg 61

Keeping Ex-Offenders Free!
An Aftercare Guide

Donald Smarto

Baker Books

A Division of Baker Book House Co
Grand Rapids, Michigan 49516

© 1994 by Donald Smarto

Published by Baker Books
a division of Baker Book House Company
P.O. Box 6287, Grand Rapids, MI 49516–6287

Printed in the United States of America

ISBN 0-8010-8357-5

Cataloging-in-Publication information is filed at the Library of Congress, Washington, D.C.

Unless otherwise indicated, Scripture quotations are from THE HOLY BIBLE, NEW INTERNATIONAL VERSION®. NIV®. Copyright © 1973, 1978, 1984 by International Bible Society. Used by permission of Zondervan Publishing House. All rights reserved.

Scriptures marked LB are from *The Living Bible*, copyright 1971 by Tyndale House Publishers, Wheaton, IL. Used by permission.

Scripture marked NKJV is from The New King James Version. Copyright © 1979, 1980, 1982, Thomas Nelson, Inc., Publishers.

This book is dedicated to prison evangelist Bill Glass

who has given me wise counsel as a mentor,

demonstrated love as a brother,

and encouraged me as a friend.

Contents

Acknowledgments   9

Introduction   11
1. Release Is Just the Beginning   19
2. A Place for Healing   45
3. The Old Personality in the New Creature   65
4. Who's in Charge?   79
5. Hungry for the Spotlight   103
6. Finding a Church Home   131
7. The Risk of Loving   151
8. Wise As Serpents   169
9. What Can the Church Do?   195

Appendix A: Prison Ministries   217
Appendix B: Churches Ministering in Jails
             and Prisons   219
Appendix C: Correspondence Courses   223
Appendix D: Practical and Professional Guidelines for Jail
             and Prison Ministry Volunteers   224
Notes   225

*A*cknowledgments

I wish to thank Lorraine Thompson for her assistance with this manuscript.

I also wish to express my gratitude to the following individuals for their valuable input:

Marcus Baird

David Benner

Dan Croce

Harry Greene

Don Holt

Sam Huddleston

Chuck Mathis

Manny Mill

Steve Miller

Mike Moeller

Jack Murphy

Don O'Dell

J. Michael Quinlan

Bruce Secord

David Spong

Harold Thompson

Donnell Turner

Finally, I wish to thank Dan Van't Kerkhoff, Editor/Trade Books, and Baker Book House for their commitment to prison ministry.

*I*ntroduction

E ach calendar year, more than one hundred thousand men[1] and women are released from America's prisons and return to cities and suburbs like yours and mine. Some have served their full sentence. Others have met the conditions for early release through a parole board's recommendation or had their sentence reduced under a federal court order ("in compliance with a consent decree"). Still others have been released by court order to ease the burden of institutional crowding.

Whatever the reason for their release, these people are now ex-offenders. Regardless of whether they have served their full sentence or paid their moral debt, in a legal sense they have paid their debt to society and are free to return to it.

But do these men and women return to society better or worse? And what happens to them in the months and years following their release? This is a vital question both for society and for the church, because the odds are great that the men and women who have been released from prison will return to crime. According to the Bureau of Justice Statistics, 60 percent of the people released from prison in a given year will have committed another crime within six months, and 75 percent will have returned to crime within a four-year period. For juvenile delinquents, the failure rate is much higher—80 to 85 percent.

Of particular interest to the church is that a significant proportion of the men and women released from prison each year will have become Christians while in prison. The efforts of the various prison ministries to reach inmates for Christ have reaped a rich harvest. In fact, on the basis of information gathered from chaplains and prison ministries,[2] we can conservatively estimate that some 10 percent of the hundred thousand prisoners released every year have made a decision and a commitment to follow Christ. Unfortunately, as many as 80 percent of these Christian ex-offenders never find a church home. Without friends, family, or a church support system, these men and women easily drift back into old habits, which often include crime.

What is the church's responsibility toward Christian ex-offenders? How can the church help these men and women grow spiritually as well as adapt to life "on the outside"? To a great extent, the answers to these questions comprise the issue of *aftercare*, which is the focus of this book.

God makes a difference in the lives of offenders. God uses the church as the predominant vehicle for his mercy. And an obvious solution for the problem of recidivism among Christian ex-offenders is for churches to adopt regenerated ex-offenders. But caring for ex-offenders, helping them grow and adjust, is far from a simple task; it demands wisdom, discernment, and practical understanding. This book is intended to provide practical help and guidance for helping churches face the issues and challenges inherent in a ministry of aftercare.

What Prison Does to People

For the last fifteen years I have worked with criminals. As a probation officer in both the adult and juvenile divisions, I counseled and wrote reports on more than seven hundred felony offenders representing every category of crime from burglary to murder. As the director of a residential drug and alcohol abuse program, I studied the emotional and psychological problems that contribute to criminal behavior. Today, as the administrator of the Charles W. Colson scholarship for ex-offenders at Wheaton College, I have screened and worked closely with hundreds of Christian ex-offenders.[3]

My professional experience has taught me one fact: *prison damages people.* In fact, the longer someone is incarcerated (especially more than five years), the harder it is for that person to become a whole person when released. Added to this, of course, is the reality that many people come to prison *already* damaged in one way or another, and their time in prison does little to help them heal or grow.

Much of the damage is emotional and psychological. For example, ex-offenders commonly have problems with authority—an attitude of mistrust or anger that may manifest itself as passive resistance, outright rebellion, or misuse of power. Many ex-offenders have also lost the capacity to trust others. This problem reveals itself symptomatically as paranoia. Ex-offenders often believe that people—including strangers—know they have been in prison and are watching them.

Because of the predatory environment of prison,[4] yet another common area of psychological damage is a desensitization to pain due to exposure to extreme violence in most jails and prisons. The more time a man or woman has served, the greater the likelihood that he or she has witnessed or been the victim of violence ranging from fights and theft to rape and murder.

In addition—and this is a vital point to understand—ex-offenders often do not comprehend the full extent of the emotional and psychological damage they have sustained. I would liken this damage to the posttraumatic stress syndrome often observed in Vietnam veterans. These men and women experienced severe trauma as soldiers. When they came home, in order to function, they pushed the memories, thoughts, sights, and emotions deep inside—even into their subconscious minds. Eventually they became unaware of both the experiences and of their defense mechanisms. But they continued to carry the bad memories as weighty baggage that hindered their ability to adjust to normal life.

An ex-offender's "baggage"—often a mixture of anger at authority, fear of physical and sexual abuse, and the horror of being a witness to violence—is part of what he or she carries back into the free world. Ex-offenders carry their prison baggage to their jobs, their marriages, and their relationships. Added to the weight of earlier experiences and pain, it can affect day-to-day

13

functioning and result in negative behaviors that come from both conscious and subconscious sources.

On top of all this, an inmate trying to readjust to society faces many formidable practical problems—getting a job, rebuilding a family, adjusting to changes in the outside world, even buying clothes—with few resources in terms of money, contacts, or appropriate social skills. Even the church that is helping him or her may seem strange and foreign, very different from the fellowship the ex-offender knew in prison.

No wonder the return to society may be hesitant and awkward for an ex-offender, even one who has the assurance of God's love and a solid commitment to Christ. Extremes of emotion can be expected, and old habits such as profanity, explosive anger, and manipulation are not likely to disappear right away. It is vital that the church recognize just what the inmate has been through and is going through in order to provide the kind of help that will really help the ex-offender grow and prevent him or her from falling back into old ways.

No More Games

A key question for any church seeking to adopt Christian ex-offenders is this: *How can we be sure that an ex-offender really is a born-again Christian?*

Of course, the question can be posed a different way: How do we know if *anyone* in our churches is a born-again Christian? And the answer, of course, is that we can't, although over time we can determine whether a person is exhibiting behaviors that indicate inner change.

But the question of authentic commitment to Christ is especially relevant in the case of ex-offenders because they are coming from a lifestyle that is largely based on deception and manipulation. Con games are a very big part of prison life. In fact, the games in the "joint" are only an extension of the games played on the streets. Most criminals will con, manipulate, fake, and steal in order to get ahead. And most incarcerated criminals will con, manipulate, fake, and steal in order to survive in prison or to get out of it. They are used to deceiving others, and often they deceive themselves as well. (*Denial* is likely to be a prisoner's most familiar defense mechanism.)

This behavior pattern modifies predictably after the prisoner becomes a disciple of Christ, but old habits die slowly. Even Christian ex-offenders need careful shepherding to help them stop playing games with each other and with themselves. Meanwhile, church leaders and members need to learn some ways to protect themselves from being manipulated or conned—either by authentic believers who are struggling to overcome habitual dishonesty or by enterprising nonbelievers who see Christians as an "easy mark" and professing Christ as a tool for avoiding the consequences for their actions.

Several years ago, a book titled *Games Criminals Play*[5] was in wide use among corrections professionals. (I have also observed its common use among many Christians involved in prison visitation.) Written by Bud Allen, a social scientist and behaviorist, and Diane Bosta, a teaching consultant for the California Department of Corrections, this book was helpful in alerting individuals about con games and manipulations. However, it had two distinct limitations for church use:

- It was not written from a Christian, biblical perspective.
- It does not concern itself with the aftercare phase.

This book, therefore, is aimed at complementing Allen and Bosta's work with a distinctively Christian perspective and with a particular emphasis on aftercare issues. It is not meant to create suspicion and avoidance on the part of churches but to help churches protect themselves from being conned while at the same time fostering the growth and maturity of the regenerated ex-offender. Guidelines will be presented for helping cultivate responsibility and accountability in the regenerated ex-offender.

Helping Ex-Offenders Grow

Most Christian ex-offenders come out of prison with some emotional and spiritual work to do. They need to change some of their habitual attitudes, such as resistance to authority and playing games with themselves and others. They need to learn to handle their emotions appropriately and positively—neither hiding from their feelings nor indulging them. They need to learn new ways of relating to people, and they need to attain some practical skills for making their way in the world without resorting to criminal behavior.

Eventually they must also demonstrate their commitment to Christ by actions that go beyond mere lip service. Ex-offenders, like all Christians, are called to sanctification, to seek forgiveness, and to grant forgiveness to others. This is part of authenticating one's faith. A genuine disciple of Jesus must be honest with God, honest with himself, and honest with others. Confession and forgiveness mark the road to sanctification. A large part of the church's role in ministering to the ex-offender is helping him or her move farther down that road.

The type of structure the church needs to provide ex-offenders is not unlike that provided by parental authority. Love must nurture and understand, but it must also provide boundaries, limits, and standards. The parent who never communicates values to the child, who never says no, is not helping the child grow. Without guidelines, the child drifts into an environment without boundaries and fails to develop mature values and a sense of responsibility.

Real love for ex-offenders must include discipline. But discipline does not concern itself merely with punishment. That is a common misconception. The word *discipline* has at its root the word *disciple*, which means to show people the right way through example and modeling. This is part of the church's responsibility to ex-offenders.

An important part of the nurturing and discipline churches need to provide for ex-offenders is to protect them from moving too quickly into positions of leadership and visibility in the Christian world. Too often, a deep need for affirmation and attention motivates an ex-offender to seek the spotlight of evangelism and ministry. And too often, the essential drama of a prison conversion combined with a desire to help the ex-offender will motivate other Christians to shine the spotlight too quickly. All this

16

can short-circuit or retard the process of growth toward true maturity.

This is not to say that ex-offenders should be treated as second-class Christians! But a man or woman who has been converted to Christ in prison needs time to grow before he or she has reached the level of spiritual maturity and emotional stability that should characterize a good Christian leader. Even an ex-offender who has shown dramatic growth in prison needs time and help adjusting to life on the outside, where the pressures and challenges will be quite different from those he or she faced in prison.

Perhaps the most effective method of providing that kind of parental modeling is matching each ex-offender one on one with a mature Christian mentor. Manny Mill, one of our Colson program graduates, is today the administrator of a transitional living house for ex-offenders that involves local churches in just such a mentoring program. The practice of mentoring or apprenticeship in many areas of skill is ages old. In like manner, we can mentor neophyte-Christian ex-offenders in the ways of Christian maturity. Essentially, we must be Barnabas to every Timothy coming out of prison.

The church definitely needs to play an active, vital, and reality-based role in helping the ex-offender readjust to life on the outside and continue to grow as a Christian. And this, in essence, is my purpose in writing this book. I hope to help churches:

- understand what the ex-offender is facing in trying to readjust to society and thus provide practical, balanced help
- cultivate the ex-offender's sense of accountability for personal sin and guide him toward accepting responsibility for personal behaviors
- detect and guard against ex-offender manipulations and game playing—for the protection of both the church members and the ex-offender
- assist the ex-offender in being an authentic disciple of Jesus Christ

Some names have been changed in order to protect privacy and confidentiality.

One additional word: Ex-offenders can be male or female. Both men and women commit crimes, serve prison sentences, find Christ in prison, and face the challenge of readjusting to the world outside of prison. Nevertheless, the vast majority of prisoners— 96 percent, to be exact—are male. For this reason—and to avoid the awkwardness of endless "he/shes," I have often chosen to use the male pronoun when referring to individual inmates and ex-offenders. However, the principles and the practical applications for churches apply equally to women and men.

1

Release Is Just the Beginning

Taking the Prison Out of the Prisoner

Release! That is the word that prisoners live to hear. Every inmate awaits his or her release day with eagerness. Prisoners call it "getting short"—the anticipation stage of returning to the free world.

Many prisoners hinge all their hopes on release, assuming it will bring the solution to all their problems. That is unfortunate, because being released from prison is not the cure-all that inmates think it will be. Most ex-offenders still face enormous difficulties once they have been released. They may struggle with finding employment, with handling finances, with managing relationships, and most of all, with the previous habit of making bad decisions.

The common belief that everything will be perfect after release is really self-deception and wishful thinking. Just as it took many weeks and months to adjust to the chaotic and predatory environment of prison, so the prisoner will need time to adjust to changes in culture and the demands of the free world.

Leaving prison physically is only part of the release process. It is entirely possible for an ex-offender to leave the institution yet still be confined emotionally and mentally. Being released from this inner confinement is a longer, more difficult process.

It may sound like a cliché, but it is also true: You can take the man out of the prison, but you still need to take the prison out of the man. And that applies to women, too!

A Nonrestricted Environment

One of the most basic ways that an ex-offender can remain confined on the inside is that he may have difficulty adjusting to the lack of physical confinement. For instance, someone who has been incarcerated for a long time may have trouble even crossing the street because he has lost the ability to judge the speed of an oncoming car. Living in close quarters for a period of months or years has actually altered his depth perception. This symptom will usually disappear within a week, but other consequences of physical confinement may last much longer.

One day the wife of a man who had been out of prison for more than ten years told me, "At times, it's as if he is still in a cell. He works very close to his bed. He stacks all his books and papers very neatly right next to his bed."

Even after ten years of freedom, this man was subconsciously confining himself to small spaces. He also tended to be very territorial. If his wife moved a single book or paper, his whole day could be thrown off.

Now, this particular prisoner may have been an extreme case. He had been institutionalized from the time he was a teenager and spent nearly twenty years of his adult life in prison. Nevertheless, similar difficulties in adjusting are not uncommon among ex-offenders.

Many ex-offenders have told me about feeling a sense of disorientation—both physical and mental—after their release. Physical symptoms may include loss of appetite, difficulty with concentration, and a lack of interest in goals. Sleep patterns may not coincide with the "normal world." Ex-offenders may find themselves awake at night and drowsy by day.

Other prisoners have problems with large open spaces or with crowds. Most of us take traffic jams, subway rides, and crowded city streets in stride. But a man or woman who has lived in a nine-by-twelve cell for long periods of time, especially one who has experienced the cramped mobility of lockdown (in lockdown prisoners stay in their cells twenty-three hours a day, usually a reaction to violence in the facility) or solitary confinement, can become literally terrorized by large open spaces or by the congestion of city streets, airport terminals, bus stations, or train stations.

In a way, these psychological restraints resemble the leg chains worn by elephants in the zoo. The elephants begin wearing their chains when they are small. As adults, they are powerful enough to break free from the chains, but they usually prefer to stay in place. They have adjusted and accommodated to confinement; keepers say the chains give them "a sense of security." Perhaps the same dynamic is at work with ex-offenders. At any rate, learning to live and work in a less restricted environment poses a challenge for many ex-offenders.

Culture Shock

Have you ever paid a visit to the "old neighborhood" where you grew up? If you've been away for any length of time, you may have been startled by the changes that had taken place— new shopping centers, different houses, the deterioration of some places and the remodeling of others. That's the kind of change that confronts many ex-offenders on a daily basis.

The man who has been in prison for ten or twenty years has literally missed out on a segment of history. Think about what the world must look like to a man or woman who has been locked in a cell for the past ten years or longer. Not only will the local landscape have changed, but prices for everything from bread to gas will have doubled or quadrupled. Cars and clothes will look strange, and unfamiliar gadgets will have become commonplace— microwaves, CD players, satellite dishes, digital thermometers, notebook computers! The rate of cultural change is hard enough

21

for nonprisoners to keep up with; to a freed prisoner it can be almost overwhelming.

Disappointed Expectations

One of the biggest shocks for the newly released ex-offender is the difference between what he expected and what he finds. Both what he remembers about life before prison and what he anticipates about life after release are likely to be tinged with fantasy.

Many released prisoners anticipate an ideal world: a husband or wife waiting with open arms, loving children who obey every command, a church eagerly awaiting their release, a lucrative job with respectful colleagues. But all of these are mostly fantasy.

Many ex-offenders are hoping for what visitors experience at the entrance of Disneyland. They dream of living on Main Street of Hometown, U.S.A., the turn-of-the-century setting where all the store proprietors smile and greet you warmly, where anyone can climb on the horsedrawn carriage or ride a fire engine without paying anyone or asking anyone's permission, where the atmosphere is gay, serene, and secure.

There is one basic problem with this picture, of course—it's pure fantasy. This picture of small-town life at the turn of the century is revisionist history, taking the best of a bygone era and ignoring the problems, disputes, sickness, and crime that existed then just as it exists today. It is true the proprietors smile and greet you warmly on Main Street, but that is their job. They are characters, actors, paid to do what they do. After having paid a large admission fee to enter the park, you can ride on the streetcar and fire engine for free.

Consider how this illustration compares to the unrealistic expectation of some released from prison. Because inmates have spent considerable time hoping and dreaming about release, they now have a romanticized view of the world. In this world, no one holds suspicion for ex-offenders and the church welcomes everyone.

But as one ex-offender told me with a sigh, "You learn soon after release that the world is the same as you left it . . . diapers still smell, your parents have the same irritating habits, and not everyone is glad you've returned!"

Family Readjustments

Ex-offenders who have families may be especially eager to return home, but at this point they may receive a shock.

In the first place, they may not have a family to return to. David Spong, the director of J.O.Y. Ministries in Wisconsin, specializes in marriage seminars with prisoners. He tells me, "Half of all inmate marriages will end up in divorce in the first year." Overall the number of divorces is higher than 80 percent.

Even if the family is still intact, a number of forces may contribute to tension at home. During the years of incarceration, the inmate and other family members may have grown apart emotionally, and husbands and wives may have lost the sense of intimacy that comes from living together on a day-to-day basis. Anger, blame, and resentment stemming from the arrest or the events that led up to it may have been festering, and there has been little opportunity to work through these problems while the inmate was incarcerated.

Inmates may encounter a lot of resistance as they attempt to reassert authority in the home. For example, a male ex-offender may be eager to take his place as head of the home, but his wife may have other ideas. After all, she has been running the household and raising the children alone. She has been responsible for paying bills, arranging for car repairs, fixing household items, filing income tax forms, and giving the children guidance. Her response to a husband who is ready to take charge again may imply, *We have done pretty well without you. We don't need your leadership.* (She may also be thinking, *His bad decisions have already caused the family trouble.*)

A female inmate may encounter similar resistance from her husband or other family members who have been raising her children. It's understandable, but it can also be painful for everyone involved.

On top of these "normal" difficulties stemming from separation, the experience of prison itself may contribute to marital problems after release. Remember, the prisoner has lived in an extremely abnormal environment. He has endured forced celibacy, and he has been exposed to considerable homosexual behavior. Even if he has not participated, he has witnessed a substantial perversion of God's laws. This cannot help but have an impact on his close relationships after he has been released.

Adding to the pressure of these adjustments is the fact that any other problems an inmate develops in adjusting to life "on the outside" will be felt most keenly at home. When an ex-offender is territorial with his possessions, paranoid about how the neighbors or relatives are watching him, seething with repressed anger about what happened to him, or grandiose about his plans or prospects, it is the family that feels the brunt of these maladjustments.

Decision Overload

Jim was an ex-offender friend of mine who had finally been released from prison after more than nineteen years behind bars. To celebrate I took him to an Italian restaurant. When the waitress came to take our order, he still had the large menu in front of his face. She came back several minutes later, but he was still contemplating the menu. When she came back the third time, I grew uncomfortable; maybe he couldn't read.

"Jim," I asked, "Is there a problem?" He slowly put down the menu and said with tears in his eyes, "It's been so long since I've had choices."

You and I might not find a large restaurant menu a formidable challenge. But then you and I are used to making hundreds of choices on a daily basis. From waking to sleep, the average citizen makes hundreds of choices ranging from the mundane ("Should I get dressed before or after breakfast?") to the important ("Should I return his phone call or wait until he calls again?") to the life-changing ("Should I stay at this job or start my own business?"). Even the cereal aisle in the grocery store presents an amazing array of possibilities. Adjusting to the number of decisions a person in ordinary society is expected to make can be one of the most difficult transitions a newly released ex-offender must make.

A newly released prisoner has essentially had no control over his own life for a period of years. Almost all his decisions have been made for him by the prison administration, and so he has little recent experience in making responsible choices. Soon after release, some inmates, simply out of habit, will ask friends and family for permission to use the telephone or even the bathroom.

The whole prison system, in fact, is set up to discourage decision making. Prisoners are told when to wake up, when to shower, what to wear, and when to move from one location to another. At day's end, the facility decides what time the lights will go out. Phone calls and visitations are strictly controlled.

The inmate can choose to rebel, but he will bear the consequences—whatever punishment the administration believes is appropriate. And if the rebellion is severe, the punishment may entail the one thing the inmate dreads most: a longer sentence. Most prisoners will do almost anything to avoid jeopardizing their chances for release, so they tend to go along, however grudgingly, with what they are told to do.

The longer someone is in an institution, the more comfortable he becomes with the lack of decisions. The inmate just eats, sleeps, and goes with the flow; he has become accustomed to not having any options. We call this "institutionalization."

In my view, one of the great problems with our American prison system is that it does not cultivate responsible decision making in the inmate. It is easy for prisoners to become institutionalized or dependent on others to make decisions for them. The obvious problem comes when they are released and expected to make a hundred responsible decisions a day. A prisoner who has been incarcerated for a period of time has no frame of reference and is likely to feel completely overwhelmed.

This is an area where an ex-offender needs to be patient with himself, and the church needs to be patient with him. It will take time and careful discipling to bring him to the point where ordinary decision making feels normal and comfortable again, and he is equipped to make responsible decisions.

That Prison "Look"

Personal appearance is another area in which ex-offenders may remain confined by a prison mentality.

I interview many ex-offenders for the Colson scholarship at Wheaton College, and I see many who by appearance alone seem to still be confined in prison. This mental confinement often translates into their choice of clothes and hairstyles, their personal hygiene, and their body language.

Granted, most ex-offenders hardly have resources to invest in new clothes, but even the way clothes are worn can demonstrate whether they are attempting to fit in or trying to label themselves as distinct and separate from the community.

Some ex-offenders move with what I would refer to as a strut—a slow walk that seems to carry an air of arrogance. It is almost militaristic. The head is held up high, the eyes are squinty, there is rarely a smile, and the shoulders are held erect with the chest pushed out. The body language seems to say "Look at me, I own this place!" or "This is my sidewalk, get out of the way!" Ex-offenders may not even be conscious that they are doing this. It's the way they walked for many years down the main hallway or "boulevard" of the prison.

Another common ex-offender "look" is to roll the shirt sleeves to the shoulder and expose the biceps. A tattoo, perhaps hand-done in the cell, may adorn the upper arm. If the ex-offender has worked with weights, as most inmates do, he probably has an impressive set of muscles. Some ex-offenders walk with their shirts open or off to show off even more tattoos and muscles.

All this display had great meaning in the prison environment. Just as a dog might protect itself by showing its teeth and growling, an inmate learns to show off his "toughness" to impress would-be attackers. But it does not make any sense to show muscles and tattoos on a suburban street or in a church setting. A man can hardly remove tattoos from his hand or other prominent places, but he does not have to go out of his way to show them. Such a display, combined with the strut, adds to the overall picture of a man who is still confined within his mind.

Society holds up basic standards of hygiene and grooming that determine what is normal or acceptable, and these standards are not hard to meet. It takes very few resources to get an occasional haircut and to use a comb in between visits to the barber. It takes relatively little time to polish shoes, even when one cannot afford a new pair. I have met many ex-offenders who look like they just walked off the cell block and into a local church. Their clothes are shabby and unkempt, and their hair looks like they just woke up. All this sends the message that the ex-offender is not trying to fit into the culture.

Many prisoners are in need of dental care. Missing teeth are as common as tattoos. I'm not suggesting that it should be a priority for someone just out of prison to run to the dentist and get a bridge, but I have met ex-offenders who, fifteen years after their release, are still displaying their missing teeth as badges of honor.

I don't want to put too much emphasis on appearance here. Uncombed hair, a rolled-up sleeve, a chipped tooth, even a tattoo may in themselves be inconsequential to the growth of the ex-offender. If the ex-offender is regenerated in Christ, however, and intends to take his place in the church and in society, at some point he should begin to look like the new person he is trying to become. Part of interpersonal accommodation—living in society and living with different people in the church—is making an attempt to fit in. In addition, the ex-offender "look" may be a symptom of an inner attitude that needs changing. Sometimes it is a conscious or unconscious challenge to society, a way of demanding, "Take me the way I am." In other cases it is a more direct expression of hostility.

Some prisoners, especially those convinced of their own status as victims of injustice, harbor deep resentment and anger toward society, but they cannot initiate retaliation or revenge while in the prison system, especially if their release date is looming. Some may express their resentment after their release, and church people become easy targets for this kind of acting out.

Many ex-offenders refer to naive church people as "squares," and some like to play a game called "Scare the Squares." Scaring the squares essentially means intimidating someone through your physical appearance, through their knowledge of your past, or both. Some ex-offenders, including some who have affirmed a new life in Christ, appear to enjoy this game and the power it gives them over people. In these cases, taking pride in an intimidating presence or using it to give others a hard time is really an indication of spiritual immaturity.

Many ex-offenders are unsuccessful in finding jobs precisely because of their appearance. As psychologist and author Ned Rollo once said, "Gorillas don't get jobs even in a zoo." He meant that people are rarely going to get a job if they scare the people they want to work for.

An example from zoology makes for an interesting comparison. One might say that looks do not mean anything, but a significant amount of human communication is done through body language as opposed to words. Nowhere is this more true than in the animal kingdom where there are no words at all—just sounds, such as growls, and appearances.

As an illustration, consider two animals, the giant panda or the gray wolf. Which one would you rather encounter in your backyard? Which one seems most threatening or menacing? Most people, judging by appearance, would find the panda cuddly and lovable and the wolves a little frightening. But this appearance can be deceiving.

A staff member at the National Zoo in Washington, D.C., once helped explain to me that the panda "appears" cute and cuddly because its round ears and short nose contribute to a babylike expression. The wolf, on the other hand, has a pointed snout, pointed ears, and sharp canine teeth that combine to give it a fierce expression. The reality is that pandas are more hostile to humans than wolves! Looks can be deceiving.

An ex-offender who walks into a job interview with rolled-up sleeves and no tie is sending a message to the interviewer. Tight lips, a squinty stare, a macho strut send a similar message. The ex-offender appears to still be in prison. Even if he is rehabilitated, he still *looks* threatening.

One of the reasons convicted serial killer Ted Bundy eluded the police for so long was that his appearance didn't proclaim "criminal." He was articulate, well mannered, good-looking, and he wore neat, preppy clothes. Bundy did not fit the stereotype of a serial killer. It was easy for him to kill because his victims found him approachable. He was finally caught because of his compulsive behavior, not his appearance.

The opposite may hold true for the ex-offender. He may be growing in Christ and honestly seeking to change his life. He may have sought forgiveness for his sins and be dedicated to rebuilding his life, but if he still looks like a prisoner, he will have a hard time earning the trust of those around him and fitting into society.

The Habit of Denial

One of the most persistent and unhealthy lingering effects of imprisonment for many prisoners is the habit of denial. Proverbs 28:13 says,

> He who conceals his sins does not prosper,
> but whoever confesses and renounces them finds mercy.

But the typical man or woman who is arrested for committing a crime is inclined neither to confess nor to renounce the behavior that got him or her in trouble in the first place.

More commonly, people who are arrested for wrongdoing fall into a pattern of denial that can continue through to the time of their release. Some consciously conceal their sins. Others actually end up deceiving themselves. Many persist in simply failing to face the reality of their behavior. Whatever form it takes, the pattern of denial blocks healing because it tends to create a victim mentality and to keep the offender from accepting responsibility for what he has done. Because denial is usually deep-seated and harmful, I want to trace the way it operates in a typical prisoner's mind throughout the process of arrest, trial, and imprisonment. In all of this discussion, I am talking of the inmate who is *actually guilty* of the crime for which he is arrested. I am aware that it is possible for an innocent man or woman to be arrested, convicted, and even imprisoned. However, I am convinced it happens far less often than movies and TV—or the inmates themselves—would lead us to believe.

Over the last ten years I have visited more than 275 prisons, and I have heard more than a thousand inmates tell me they are

29

innocent of the crimes for which they were convicted. While it is certainly possible for an innocent person to be convicted, there cannot possibly be as many innocent prisoners as those who protest their innocence. All too often, claiming to be innocent becomes just another form of denial, a mind game that keeps the offenders from confessing and renouncing their sins, so as to obtain mercy.

Denial of the Crime

"There was a time," remembers the psalmist, "when I wouldn't admit what a sinner I was. But my dishonesty made me miserable and filled my days with frustration" (Ps. 32:3 LB). This in essence is what denial does to the offender at every step along the way.

The first denial is of the crime itself. As I have mentioned, many offenders will claim to be totally innocent of the charges, even when overwhelming evidence points to their guilt. Another form of denying the crime is to fall into rationalizations and excuses. The most common excuse is that of "being in the wrong place at the wrong time." Another is blaming other people: "I was with Butch, and I didn't know what he was doing. Before I knew it, he was holding up the gas station and there I was."

Denial of crime also includes attempting to reduce one's culpability and the severity of the crime. For instance, a rapist may insist, "I thought she wanted it." Or the perpetrator of a violent crime may say, "I didn't really think I was hurting him." An armed robber may say, "I only wanted to scare him. I really didn't think the gun was loaded." I have even heard murderers say, "I didn't think I hit him that hard; I only wanted to teach him a lesson."

In each case, the offender admits he was there and did something. It is really a form of denial to make excuses for the crime or to try to lessen the severity of it.

Several years ago I was reviewing the application of an ex-offender to the Wheaton College program. In his statement of accountability he said he received a nineteen-year sentence for burglary, his first offense. I know sentencing guidelines, and I knew his claim was preposterous! He must have been charged and found guilty of something far greater than a first-offense burglary. So I called him, hoping he would, of his own initiative, give me more information. He did not. He only repeated the same story. I am convinced that, with repetition, he had come to believe it himself. Eventually, I simply commented, "I don't believe you got nineteen years just for burglary. Why did the judge say he was sending you to prison?" He blurted, "Kidnapping! But she wasn't supposed to be there!"

He explained further that the woman who owned the house was to have been working at the hour he planned his burglary. She had called in sick that day. When he entered the house, he discovered her and subsequently kidnapped her. Most people would readily agree that kidnapping is a very serious offense, but this man's perception was different. In his mind, he was only a burglar.

This man had been out of prison for more than five years after serving eight years. Yet he still was not accepting responsibility for what had really brought him to prison. He was blaming the victim and unpredictable circumstances for his crime. In essence, he was still playing a game.

A prisoner who combs through the law books looking for a technical error in his court case is also playing a game. In his heart, he knows he is guilty of the crime, but he can expend so much effort trying to win his freedom that he becomes convinced of his own innocence. Even after release he can turn his entire incarceration experience into an injustice.

Denial of Arrest

An arrest means that a police officer bodily places you in a police car and takes you to a jail. It is a very intrusive process. You are handcuffed. Someone reads you your Miranda rights. Officers will use as much force as is necessary to take you into custody; they have the legal authority to do that if there is reasonable belief that you have committed a crime. The more you resist, the more officers will be needed and the more force will be used.

On arriving at the jail, the booking process begins. An officer takes your statement. Your hand is inked for fingerprinting. You are told where to stand for a mug shot. You are searched—probably strip-searched.

31

It would seem that only someone who is out of touch with reality could hang on to denial during all this. Denial at this stage typically takes the form of statements like "You got the wrong person!" or "This is some terrible mistake" or "Why are you doing this? I don't deserve this!" That would be the normal reaction for an innocent person. For the person who knows he has committed a crime, this stage of denial requires amazing mental gymnastics—and many offenders manage it.

Within the first few hours after arrest, the offender is allowed to make a phone call. As he desperately dials a family member or friend, his preoccupation at this stage is typically not with the crime committed and the predictable consequences but "What can you do to get me out?" An offender will beg family or friends to come down to the jail with money for bail. If bail is set too high, the next plea is for a good attorney. Short of the arraignment (the hearing when charges are announced), there really is not much an attorney can do, certainly not in the first few hours. Yet offenders will call an attorney at any hour, even midnight, hoping for immediate release. While this behavior is not unusual, even for the guilty, it is the beginning of the preoccupation with "beating a case"—escaping consequences even on a technicality.

Some trials, especially in cases of major crimes, can take a long time, even one to three years. The individual can sit in jail all that time, especially if no bond is set. Yet many offenders after more than a year still say, "I can't believe I'm in jail. I don't deserve to be here." This is not so much a denial of the physical incarceration as a denial of the behaviors that brought them there.

Denial of the Finding of Guilt

By the time a jury or judge finally enters a guilty verdict, quite a lot of time may have elapsed. Most of this time has been consumed by preparation for a trial. The offender has consulted with his attorney, either a private attorney or one appointed through the public defender's office. Hopefully, the attorney has made a valiant defense, but in the mind of the jury there has been overwhelming evidence to convince them the individual accused is guilty.

Guilt is typically determined not only on the basis of eyewitness testimony but also by physical evidence, which by today's standards is usually highly scientific and very accurate. Forensic scientists can do much more than match footprints, tire prints, and fingerprints. Bullets can be traced to a specific gun. Marks from a window that has been forced open can be matched to a specific screwdriver. Fibers from a piece of tape can be identified as coming from a specific roll. Clothing fibers found at the scene of a crime can be traced to an article of clothing, and teeth marks on a victim can even be matched to a particular set of teeth.

Even in the face of overwhelming evidence, the offender typically remains hopeful that his attorney can get him off. So naturally, when the finding of guilt is read in open court, the offender falls easily into another form of denial: "If I had had a better attorney, I would have gotten off." During this stage of denial the offender may also blame relatives for not coming up with enough cash to pay for a "really good attorney."

A minority defendant might also be inclined to use racism as the reason for conviction. For instance, an African-American may scan an all-white jury and assume "If I had had a jury of my own race, I wouldn't have been found guilty." Sadly, racial prejudice does exist in our criminal justice system, but it's also true that an accusation of racism can be an easy excuse. When employed by someone who knows he is guilty of a crime, it becomes just another tool of denial.

In our adversarial legal system, the result of a trial is winner take all. That means that if the prosecution wins, the defendant loses. He loses everything, including his freedom, when he is convicted. If there is any room for bargaining, it took place before the trial. Now there is very little room in which to negotiate. The offender had pinned all his hopes on a finding of innocent. Denial at this stage takes the form of "I can't believe I was found guilty"—sometimes combined with "when I am innocent."

Denial of Prison

After the finding of guilt a judge imposes a sentence. In certain felony cases, state legislators have mandated the sentencing, so the judge has very little discretion. In other instances, the judge

33

has some discretion to impose sentencing but still must work within sentencing guidelines that have been suggested by decisions by the state Supreme Court and by the United States Supreme Court. A judge cannot arbitrarily sentence someone to five years in prison for jaywalking, any more than he could arbitrarily give six months of incarceration for a homicide.

What this means is that the sentencing after a finding of guilt is rather predictable. Witnesses may be called to explain aggravating and mitigating circumstances, and at this stage the defendant may still believe he is going to "get off."

In one sense, of course, there may be more than simple denial in that expectation, for it is true that many people who commit crimes in America do not go to prison. According to the Bureau of Crime Statistics in Washington, D.C., one out of every three crimes committed nationwide is brought to police attention. Only one in five of the crimes being investigated—or only seven out of a hundred crimes—results in an arrest. Although 80 to 90 percent of prosecuted felonies result in a conviction, statistically only half are incarcerated. That means that upon sentencing, a defendant has a 50 percent chance of being put on probation.

So when a judge actually does hand down a prison sentence—usually because of the seriousness of the crime or a past pattern of unsuccessful probation—the defendant is almost always shocked. First, he can't believe he fell into the 50 percent of offenders that did not get probation. Second, he probably realizes that his sentence could have been very different had he committed the crime in a different place or even drawn a different judge.

Depending on what county or state the defendant resides in, sentences can vary widely. I have talked with inmates in Texas prisons who are serving seven-year sentences for auto theft. In Chicago, a criminal would have to steal a fleet of cars before he would see the inside of a prison. The institutions in Illinois are so overcrowded that space has to be reserved for the violent offenders. In one sense, then, a defendant is unlucky when arrested in Dallas for auto theft as opposed to Chicago.

Judges, too, vary in the way they hand down sentences. Some judges become known as "hanging judges," sometimes simply because they believe in punishment and consequences. But this of course can set the stage for more denial. "If I hadn't gotten that judge, I wouldn't have gone to prison," the offender says. During this stage, the blame is shifted from the poor attorney and the prejudiced jury to the heartless judge. Instead of concentrating on what behaviors brought him into the court, the offender chooses to focus on the "unfairness" of the system and the judge who was "out to get me!"

This whole process of denial only serves to reduce the offender's culpability in his own eyes. More and more, he perceives himself as a victim of the system.

Denial of the Actual Prison Term

Most prisoners do not "put up the curtains"—that is, consider prison home—for nearly a year. In the meantime, the process of denial continues.

During the first year, the offender may cling to the hope that his attorney will win his release on an appeal. He may even expect a miracle—that the governor's office will call with clemency or the commutation of a sentence.

When the realization finally comes, as it eventually does, that no attorney is working feverishly day and night to get him released, the inmate often turns to a "jailhouse lawyer"—an inmate who helps other inmates with legal paperwork—to begin the process of sending out writs and appeals. A famous appeal by a man named Gideon who lived in Florida nearly thirty years ago established a precedent for courts to consider such petitions drawn by inmates. However, unless there is overwhelming evidence that a person was wrongfully committed to prison, he must simply "do his time."

Denial after Release

As we have seen, many offenders adopt a pattern of ongoing denial from the very beginning of their encounter with the law. How does this stubborn refusal to see and acknowledge reality affect an inmate's life after release? If he has spent most of his time before and during his incarceration denying the reality of his circumstances, the events around him, and especially his guilt and culpability, the pattern of denial is likely to continue after his release, especially as he encounters difficult circumstances.

This ongoing denial can take the form of blaming others for problems. Instead of taking responsibility for what he has done and what he needs to do, the ex-offender claims that the church, his family, and the local community are at fault for not helping him get a job, not accepting him the way he wants to be accepted, not supporting a grandiose scheme to begin a ministry.

In addition, the ex-offender may persist in claiming his innocence or excusing his previous behavior. If denial of what he has done occupied much of his thinking while he was caught up in the criminal justice process, it can also occupy much of his time after release. He may even become preoccupied with "setting the record straight."

What many ex-offenders need after release is reality therapy. They must be helped to see the real obstacles to transition and adjustment, the need for patience in finding a job, redefining their relationships, and setting realistic goals for the future. Churches can encourage this realistic view by getting the facts about the ex-offender's situation and then refusing to play along with his denial. Mature, responsible church mentors can really impact the ex-offender in setting reasonable and realistic goals, but patience and caring shouldn't mean gullibility. Without denouncing or accusing, it is still possible to confront a former prisoner gently when he falls into denial or blaming someone else for his own mistakes.

Bargaining, Manipulation, and Playing Games

Even when prisoners are not caught in the insidious habit of denying reality, they are usually caught up in some form of game-playing or manipulation. Often the desire to cut corners or to get something for nothing is the motive for the crime in the first place, and once the arrest has occurred the offender is often on the lookout for ways to manipulate the system and escape his rightful punishment.

Bargaining to Lessen the Sentence

Once an offender is arrested, for example, he may do everything he can to reduce the consequences of his own crime, perhaps by offering to be a witness for the prosecution against his co-defendants. He may agree to be "wired" with a hidden microphone to record conversations from drug dealers or even to set up a drug deal in which other offenders will be trapped. In return for this "help," he hopes that police or the prosecution may be persuaded to drop charges.

Obviously, this "cooperation" is usually based on selfish motives. The offender is usually not concerned about what happens to others; he is just watching out for himself. I know of many cases in which offenders make up stories about other people's crimes in order to reduce their own sentences. Sometimes prisoners are even paid to inform on their cellmates, although such testimony is usually considered questionable. Working with the police or the prosecution in this way often sets up a pattern in which the offender is willing to manipulate others to lessen his own sentence.

Entering a Plea Agreement

The plea agreement is a legal version of "Let's Make a Deal," and it, too, encourages game-playing and manipulation on the part of the offender. A particular defendant may be charged on several separate counts or degrees of the crime. His guilt on those charges has to be proved in court, and court time costs the state a considerable amount of time and money, and there is always the chance that the prosecution might lose. So the state often offers to drop some of the charges if the offender pleads guilty on several of the counts (usually the more serious ones).

At other times, especially when the prosecution feels its case is weak, it may reduce a charge in return for a guilty plea. A charge of drunken driving may be reduced to reckless driving, for example, or the charge of homicide may be reduced to involuntary homicide.

Such an arrangement is a compromise, and usually both sides win something in the deal. The prosecution gets a conviction but not on every charge. The offender is pronounced guilty and has a punishment assessed, but it will not be as severe as it would have been had he been convicted of all charges or the more serious charge.

The nature of plea bargaining can easily open up more opportunities for manipulation on the part of the offender. For instance, if the charge of armed robbery gets reduced to one simple robbery as part of a plea bargain, that means the violent portion of the crime has been removed from the final charge and the ultimate sentence. The offender may then tell people after release, "I was never a violent offender." Technically, his statement is true, but morally it is a lie.

The plea agreement is most harmful to the offender when he comes to believe that he is only as guilty as the lesser plea implies. An alcoholic with a repeated pattern of driving under the influence, for instance, may repeatedly endanger the lives of pedestrians or other motorists. As part of a plea bargain, however, he may end up being convicted of reckless driving, which amounts to no more than going over a double yellow line. Consequently he may end up relabeling his own crime, convincing himself that his offense was just not that bad.

Playing the Probation Game

Most criminals think of probation as "getting off," and they've got a point. In the large cities of America, probation basically involves a quick monthly visit to a probation officer who is overworked and has little chance of demanding true accountability from the probationer. I know of probation officers who are assigned more than a hundred cases at a time—virtually an unmanageable caseload. There is scarcely time within the fifteen minutes allotted for a visit for the probation officer to verify the place of employment, residence, or other basic information. In many larger cities probation officers have told me that they actually lose track of many probationers.

Having been a probation officer myself, I recall from experience that most offenders on probation play a game. They want everything to look okay, so they give minimal answers. It is difficult for the probation officer to act as a counselor when the man on probation is thinking only, "Did he buy it?" or "I got through this month."

Because of these dynamics, probation basically means that the offender has returned to the streets, maybe doing everything he was doing before, but checking in fifteen minutes a month with "some square who's basically out of it." Unless the probation takes the form of an intensive supervision, which requires frequent meetings and includes more restrictive conditions such as periodic imprisonment or work release, for all practical purposes, the individual on probation is free.

There is also a vast communication network among offenders. They tell each other how to look before a judge, how to con a probation or parole officer, and what minimum tasks they need to perform to keep from being considered in violation of their parole agreement.

Many offenders have discovered that simply disappearing is often the best way of manipulating the criminal justice system. Unless someone has been convicted of a very serious felony, states do not have the time or resources to bring people back who have left the state. If someone in the state of Illinois simply moves to Michigan and adopts a new social security number and an alias, the chances of his being discovered are very small.

Police solve most crimes by looking in the general area for possible subjects. Various jurisdictions and states will not work together to arrest a misdemeanor offender. Criminals know this and utilize this simple technique of drifting to avoid being caught.

The game actually does not work as well as the probationers think it does. Most probation officers are smart enough to know if there is a con going on. Arrests or convictions in other states are immediately discovered because of the computerization of a driver's license. In fact, one-half to two-thirds of those going to prison are sent because they violated the conditions of their probation or parole. Those who elude probation but commit no new crimes that result in arrest often escape the system. When I was a probation officer, for example, one of my clients was a man who had committed a serious sexual felony. One of the conditions of probation declared that the offender could not leave the state (in this case, Illinois) without the probation officer's permission. One day

I got word that this man had been arrested in Iowa for public intoxication—not a huge offense but clear evidence that he had violated the conditions of his probation. His probation was revoked, and he was resentenced on the original offense, receiving a ten-year prison term.

When an offender is successful at playing the probation game, he learns that rules are there to be manipulated. The mindset of escaping responsibility and putting one over on the authorities is a given throughout the criminal justice system.

Surviving in a Manipulative Environment

Going to prison is like going to another planet in the cultural sense, and most inmates survive by learning to play the prison game. Prison is basically a microcosm of street life, only more intensified. Values are turned upside down, especially from the Christian perspective. Love is viewed as weakness and one-upmanship becomes power. Deception, tricks, and backstabbing are standard operating procedures. Inmates soon learn they can trust no one, that even a friend may deceive them, and that anyone seen as getting too friendly with the guards or administration may be perceived as an informer.

The inmate, therefore, tends to isolate himself, and he learns to hold his own in the prison culture through bravado and manipulation. "War stories," in which inmates tell each other about the crimes they did on the outside, are a big part of the prison culture, and these stories quickly become exaggerated. It doesn't take long for an inmate imprisoned for writing bad checks to be bragging about the people he has killed.

A very nice couple who were prison ministry volunteers recently asked me if I thought the prisoner they were ministering to was exaggerating. The inmate claimed to be in prison for murder and explained, "My mother was coming home from shopping and was jumped by a gang. They began to rape her. One by one I pulled them off and stabbed each gang member until I had killed all of them!"

I smiled gently at the couple and then said, "I find that story hard to believe." Could it have happened? Possibly. Did it happen? Probably not.

More likely, what actually happened was a single individual attacked the offender's girlfriend. This inmate had probably repeated the exaggerated story numerous times in the prison, to the point that he had begun to believe it himself. The story evolved in the telling: The girlfriend gradually became his mother and the single attacker turned into ten. After all, killing someone while defending your mother from multiple rape sounds a lot more noble than just protecting your girlfriend or, even worse, killing someone as part of a robbery attempt.

All war stories tend to have two effects. First, they make the story teller sound stronger and more dangerous, an impression that may help protect him in prison. Second, the war story can actually lessen his sense of culpability in the crime. In this case, his crime was not the murder of an innocent person but the murder of people who were viciously attacking his mother. War stories start as exaggerations and ultimately become lies.

An offender may also engage in a pattern of lies to his family and others who care about him. A prisoner can be depressed or fearful but he tells the family, "Things are going great!" He may think he is protecting them from hurt, but he has probably also fallen prey to the accepted practice among prisoners of deceit, manipulation, and covering up. In the process, unfortunately, he has stripped himself of the most valuable support system he has. The prisoner may actually tell himself that he is okay and that prison life "isn't so bad." He lies to others, to his family, and to himself. Progressively, he falls into a pattern of deception, which will last throughout his imprisonment and possibly carry over to his life after release.

The Letter-Writing Campaign

Another common form of manipulation used by some offenders is to appeal to the church and "all softhearted people" to come to his rescue. Many of these letters cross my desk each month. One, from a prisoner named Jay, pleaded, "Please address your congregation concerning this letter. I need all the backing and support I can. And I can turn to no one else except the church. *Please! I am innocent.* Please, give me your phone number and let me call you collect so I can explain the situation to you in detail."

A chaplain friend of mine knew Jay. He told me he was in fact guilty as charged, and he had a long criminal history as well. He was not a member of any church—he only claimed to be a Christian—but he had now become obsessed with sending out letters to churches hoping that they would come to his rescue. Once he managed to engage people in phone conversations, Jay asked them to give him money, send it to his family, or deposit money in an account outside the prison. He also asked people to write letters to the parole board.

A letter-writing campaign like Jay's is just another form of bargaining with the system. The inmate finally realizes he cannot get what he wants from the courts, so he attempts to get it through individual citizens and the church.

With very little real information about a case, individuals in churches have come to the rescue of inmates. Based on the sincerity of the offender's voice and the plaintiveness of his letters, volunteers have started writing to legislators, judges, and parole boards. When churches and church people do this, they are usually falling right into the hands of a skilled manipulator.

An Ongoing Habit of Manipulation

After release, unfortunately, the ex-offender is likely to continue with habits of manipulation and game-playing. For instance, he usually meets with a parole officer, and he often plays a game similar to the one he plays with the probation officer. The ex-offender tells the parole officer what he thinks will convince him that he is doing fine. If the officer probes, the ex-offender shuts himself off.

If the offender resides in a Christian halfway house, transitional home, or is sponsored by a church while on parole, he is likely to bring the mindset of game-playing, bargaining, and manipulation into the local church. The ex-offender can easily use people to get jobs and to get ahead without making a serious commitment to becoming a responsible member of society and of the church.

Game-playing is often used where money is concerned. Ex-offenders will buy mailing lists, print business cards with a ministry name, and send out appeals for support, claiming that "God told me to do this!" One game is to send appeal letters citing a created crisis.

How does the habit of manipulation contribute to the ex-offender's being confined on the outside? Clearly patterns of bargaining and game-playing confirm a deeply ingrained habit of dishonesty. Even though the ex-offender is out of prison, he may continue to play con games and tell elaborate war stories. (In a church setting, these may take the form of embellished and exaggerated personal testimonies.)

This in turn can play havoc with an ex-offender's relationships, his self-image, his spiritual well-being, and even his future. It's hard to grow emotionally and spiritually when you're stuck in the habit of playing games and looking for easy ways out. It's hard to learn to cope with real life when you have developed patterns of avoiding responsibility through bargains and "deals."

Helping Ex-Offenders Break Free

For most inmates, getting out of prison involves much more than walking out the prison gates. No matter how eagerly it is anticipated, life on the outside will require some adjustment. How can the church help the ex-offender become released from the prison within his mind as well as from his physical prison? Here are some suggestions:

1. We can be patient as the ex-offender adjusts to the shock of a new environment and works at making responsible decisions.
2. We can help the ex-offender be patient with himself, to realize that release is not the solution to all the problems of his life.
3. We can provide the opportunity for personal and family counseling through pastoral contacts and financial support.
4. In a kind way, if necessary, we can help the ex-offender adjust his appearance. This goes beyond the simple donation of clothes. A mentor who can give feedback about the way the former inmate looks, walks, and dresses is helpful.
5. We can assist him in a lifestyle of honesty before God, in his relationships, and with himself by refusing to be manipu-

lated, confronting him gently when he falls into patterns of deception, and continuing to love and accept him throughout the process.

6. We can pray for him and for his ongoing growth.

Overall, church, family, and friends of an ex-offender should hang on to both patience and hope. It is important to realize and accept that some of the psychological effects of long-term incarceration may be part of the ex-offender's behavior patterns for a long time. But it is also vital to keep in mind that real growth is possible through the power and grace of God.

As Paul put it in Romans 8:31: "What, then, shall we say in response to this? If God is for us, who can be against us?"

2

A Place for Healing

Helping the Ex-Offender
Overcome Emotional Damage

For many ex-offenders, returning to the free world after release from prison is like trying to board a moving train! Everything in the world is moving fast—cars, people, computer screens, computer games. Even life in the local church seems to proceed at breakneck speed—meetings, schedules, agendas, committees, councils, forums, things to do and people to meet.

The key phrase in the free world—and in the church as well—is "hurry up!" But to an ex-offender who had endless time on his hands in prison, who could lie on his bunk for hours, adjusting to this new tempo is no easy task.

Prison schedules are very predictable: now you eat, now the lights go out, now you shower. The key word in prison is *wait*. Wait for the guards. Wait to be searched. Wait to enter the visitation room. Wait for a parole hearing. Wait for a release date.

Nothing waits in the rapid free world; the ex-offender either gets on board or the world passes by. This is the initial challenge for most newly released prisoners. And it is this desire to catch up that creates many early problems.

The first forty-eight hours to three months is when most ex-offenders fail, reverting to old habits. This time of adjustment is both traumatic and crucial. Bad decisions in the first weeks and months can lead to depression, a return to crime, and a return to prison. This is a time when the church's role is extremely important.

Behind from the Beginning

For many ex-offenders, actually, the need to catch up involves much more than just time lost in incarceration and the need to adjust to a faster schedule. While prisoners represent all races, socio-economic classes, and levels of education, consider a profile of the typical prisoner in America:

- The average prisoner is young—twenty-four years of age.
- The vast majority come from broken homes.
- Authority and discipline in the average prisoner's life has been inconsistent and often abusive.
- The average prisoner has dropped out of school by ninth grade.
- The average prisoner functions at a fourth- or fifth-grade reading level.
- The average prisoner has been a victim of injustice during arrest, prosecution, sentencing, imprisonment—or all four.
- The average prisoner feels rejection from society.
- The average prisoner has become increasingly paranoid the longer he is incarcerated.
- The average prisoner lives in a world of forced celibacy and unnatural sexual tension.
- The average prisoner is lonely.
- The average prisoner resents authority, especially judges, police, prosecution, and guards.
- The average prisoner may feel that God has rejected him, simply does not care, or doesn't exist at all—and also thinks that church is for "squares" or for the weak.

Add all those together, and a clear picture emerges of a human being in pain—a man or woman who struggles with many negative emotions, including anger, sadness or sorrow, grief, fear, loneliness, jealousy, confusion.

As we shall see, the ex-offender may not be conscious of these feelings, but they are probably there nevertheless. They are part of the reason the ex-offender has built up such a romanticized picture of life on the outside; for months or years he has dreamed of relief from the pain. Unfortunately, these unrealistic expectations set the ex-offender up for more negative emotions as fantasy clashes with reality.

Emotional hang-ups and difficulties combined with the lack of an emotional support system can make the problem of catching up especially daunting, and many ex-offenders are tempted just to give up. For this reason, helping the ex-offender cope with the emotional aftermath of incarceration and heal from his emotional wounds is a crucial part of helping him learn to adjust to life on the outside.

How Emotions Work

Emotions are basic human reactions; we all experience them in response to what happens to us. In the most basic sense, they are protective mechanisms, designed to alert us to what is going on in our lives. In response to a threat, for instance, we feel fear or anger (or both). In response to a loved one's touch, we feel comforted and secure. In response to loss, we feel sadness and grief.

At this simplest level, feelings are neither good nor bad. They are merely alarms or responses, and even the negative ones serve a purpose—they help alert us to physical or emotional danger. In this sense, ignoring emotions can be dangerous—just as ignoring a beeping smoke alarm can be hazardous.

Although the basic experience of emotion is involuntary, there is an intricate link between the mind and the emotions—between thinking and feeling. This means that we humans can *choose* how we respond to our emotions. When we dwell on negative thoughts, we will tend to feel the emotions that accompany those thoughts.

When we choose to concentrate on positive thoughts, the emotions will tend to follow. Once we have paid attention to the signals our feelings are giving us, we can then choose to act in a responsible way that will contribute to our long-term well-being.

That, of course, is a description of how a balanced, emotionally healthy human being handles emotion. Few of us live up to that ideal—at least not all of the time. An ex-offender who has been deeply wounded before or during his prison experience will have even more difficulty reaching that emotional balance.

Because emotions can influence us in such profound ways, the process of learning to handle emotion is key to becoming healthy, productive human beings. God, through the example of Jesus and the writers of the Bible, especially the writings and teachings of the apostle Paul, has given the church strong guidelines and values for reducing negative emotions and increasing the experience of positive emotions.

That doesn't mean that Christians don't experience both negative and positive emotions like everyone else. Ex-offenders (and all Christians) will continue to get angry at people occasionally. Newly released prisoners (and all Christians) will experience sexual temptations and inappropriate passions. The possibility of choosing sinful behavior based on emotion remains.

Christians, however, have two realities in their lives that are essential for overcoming the effects of negative emotions. The first is the power and indwelling of the Holy Spirit. Without this resource, we would all be hopelessly trapped and bound to destructive passions. The second is the reality of forgiveness—both God's forgiveness of us and our forgiveness of others. With forgiveness comes healing and the ability to overcome the harmful effects of negative emotions.[1]

Emotional Side Effects of Incarceration

One ex-offender named Mike was incarcerated for more than fifteen years. Mike told me that late at night, once or twice a week, he would drive his car on rural back roads at speeds over a hundred miles an hour. Sometimes while racing he would open

48

his window and scream at the top of his lungs. Mike said this made him feel better, but he really had little insight as to why he did this.

To understand just what was happening to Mike, we must turn our attention to the incarceration experience itself. Euphemisms aside, a prisoner lives in a cage. He has been convicted and sentenced in a courtroom. He has heard derogatory comments from the prosecution and usually a stern lecture from the sentencing judge. He usually feels the wrath and rejection of society as well. To many he is "garbage" or "scum."[2] In prison, slowly but predictably, his trust of other human beings diminishes. He learns to watch his back constantly. Hope of release dominates his thoughts, and survival in the institution becomes his means to that goal. This means that all the values we hold important in the Christian community must be hidden or abated during incarceration. A prisoner cannot openly express love; he cannot be trustworthy, kind, or generous—at least, not without paying a price.

Even if the prisoner becomes a Christian while incarcerated, he is not likely to receive a lot of support for upholding Christian values. There are isolated examples of medium and minimum security facilities that have a thriving inmate Christian community, but they are usually a subculture of the larger prison population. Christianity is not the embraced religion or value system for the vast number of prisoners in large state prisons and penitentiaries.

Because the incarceration environment is so stressful, emotional side effects may plague the ex-offender for months, even years, after release.

Anger

Actions such as driving on back roads at high speeds and screaming are really symptomatic behavior. The offender has repressed the significant anger he holds against police, his lawyer, the judges, his parents, and even the church. He may even blame those who had no role in his imprisonment for not helping him to escape from his situation. After release, all this anger may show itself in eruptions of temper.

Dr. David Benner in his excellent book, *Healing Emotional Wounds,*[3] states that anger is often a response to deep feelings of loss. Undoubtedly, a prisoner experiences great loss when incarcerated. He loses his freedom and his family and many of his options. Anger is a predictable part of his grieving for the loss. Chances are he will have no opportunity to deal with that anger in a healthy way. In prison, inmates are not free to show emotion. It's no wonder that their anger grows over time.

In 1982 and 1983, Dr. Benner was a consultant to a drug and alcohol abuse program I administered. Many of the sixty individuals who went through the drug program had been incarcerated at one time or another. As a Christian clinical psychologist, Dr. Benner helped my understanding of the emotional consequences of incarceration, most specifically that of anger.

Dr. Benner explained that anger often serves as a defense mechanism. Rather than expose themselves to feelings of hurt and vulnerability associated with grief, ex-offenders defend themselves by lashing out at others. Their explosions of anger serve as a distraction from their real feelings of hurt and loss.

Anger may also be part of a pattern of denial that blames others for the prisoner's incarceration. If the offender can keep focused on his poorly skilled attorney, the vindictive cop, the overly stern judge, and the biased jury, then he does not have to deal with his feelings of frustration, loss, grief, and guilt—or the reality that he brought much of this pain on himself.

Often, the offender successfully blames the loss of his family and his freedom on the criminal justice system and society at large. If unregenerated in Christ, he may plot revenge in one form or another, even returning to crime with an escalation in violent behavior.

I once asked Dr. Benner why he thought so many of the incarcerated people I worked with seemed to have no real emotional highs or lows. Some of them seemed almost zombie-like, devoid of emotion. "The emotions of grief and loss are extremely painful," he explained, "and human beings do not tend to tolerate pain for long periods of time." This reality may help account for the prevalence of drugs in our society. We live in an era when so many people are self-medicated, some with over-the-counter drugs, some with prescription drugs, and some with illegal drugs—all in an attempt to feel good and eradicate physical, emotional, and spiritual pain.

Dr. Benner further explained that people who experience prolonged pain eventually "shut down"—cutting themselves off emotionally from the source of the pain. Unfortunately, in the process, they successfully cut off all emotions, even the good ones. They may also withdraw into themselves, becoming absorbed in their own pain and almost paralyzed with self-pity.

One thing Dr. Benner told me that I found surprising is that anger may actually serve to restore an inmate's feeling of power. Since hurt leaves people feeling vulnerable, anger may help them feel, as Dr. Benner states in his book, "a restoration of one's sense of power."

Ephesians 4:31–32 says, "Get rid of all bitterness, rage and anger, brawling and slander, along with every form of malice. Be kind and compassionate to one another, forgiving each other, just as in Christ God forgave you." For an ex-offender who has been steeped in anger for a number of years, getting rid of "bitterness, rage and anger" can be a daunting proposition. And the church is sometimes little help, because we have trouble dealing with anger, too. We cling to the myth that a growing Christian will always be kind, gentle, and moderate. Those of us in touch with reality know that is not true. But the ex-offender may often put overwhelmingly unrealistic expectations on himself to be perfect or saintly. In the process, he may be denying his anger or pushing aside negative feelings that need to be confronted.

In Scripture, the only proper anger is the kind of anger that Jesus modeled—the anger we call righteous indignation. When Jesus cleansed the temple, he was responding in righteous indignation to the defiling of his Father's temple. Jesus' anger had a higher purpose. Today, that kind of higher purpose might be found in anger over social injustice and neglect of the poor.

We are not Jesus, however, and if we are honest with ourselves we have to admit that most of our anger doesn't take the form of righteous indignation! As sinners, we get angry at times for petty reasons—and even our righteous anger may be tinged with selfishness and self-deception. We must seek forgiveness and be ready

51

to forgive, but denying our anger or pushing it under doesn't really help matters.

One of the most destructive emotional attitudes an ex-offender can adopt is the belief that he has no anger at all. An ex-offender once told me that after being released from prison he discovered that his wife had committed adultery. I asked him how he felt and he said, "Fine." I asked him if he was angry. He responded, "Angry? Of course not. I have forgiven her; there's no problem."

I was happy to hear of his ability to forgive but perplexed that he had never felt any anger regarding his wife's adultery. Adultery is basically a betrayal of a very intimate relationship. It was my belief that he had suppressed the hurt and was denying his real feelings.

The problem with such denial is that it just won't work in the long run. Anger that is denied will come out in one way or another—as depression, physical illness, or an inappropriate explosion of rage. Many ex-offenders have told me how proud they are of "telling off" a fellow church member—and in most cases their expressed anger is totally out of proportion with the offense. (In one case, the ex-offender exploded in a church meeting and the pastor actually feared for his life.)

In such cases I believe these inappropriate explosions come from trying to deny or suppress anger caused by a totally different set of circumstances. I believe there are two extreme reactions to avoid with anger. One is the total denial that we ever get angry, and the other is to repress it for long periods until it emerges in an explosive rage.

Rage or uncontrolled anger is never productive for anyone, especially not for the ex-offender. Uncontrolled anger at a police officer during a traffic stop can surely result in a bad experience— a ticket or, worse still, an arrest!

If we in the church are to help the ex-offender to full spiritual and emotional maturity, then helping him recognize and express anger appropriately will be extremely important. It may be necessary to encourage him to have counseling. The ex-offender must learn that differences of opinion and friction in relationships are normal and that feelings of anger resulting from these everyday irritations can be handled without being either repressed or expressed as rage. The ex-offender may need to learn that it really is possible to heed the admonition of Psalm 37:8: "Stop your anger! Turn off your wrath. Don't fret and worry—it only leads to harm" (LB).

Relational Difficulties

One of the primary problems that comes with either emotional shutdown or emotional explosions is the damage these imbalances can do to an ex-offender's close relationships. For example, if a married prisoner has shut off his feelings to keep from experiencing pain, he will also have difficulty expressing love, and this can wreak havoc in the prisoner's marriage. In his urgency to make up for lost time, the ex-offender may be eager to resume the sexual expression of the marriage while being unable to participate in the emotional warmth and the accompanying verbal communication.

God created the union of marriage. Essentially a spouse should be a friend in whom the other person can confide. When that spouse is nursing emotional wounds, it is difficult for him to be supportive of his partner. The spouse of an ex-offender is an injured party too. She has experienced her own brand of trauma while her husband was in prison, and in a sense she was as much a victim of his incarceration as he was. The wife has been lonely. Sexual abstinence has been forced on her also, along with the entire responsibility of keeping the family together. She has probably suffered severe financial setback as legal bills mounted, and she may have lost her home. She has certainly experienced shame and embarrassment. I know of many instances where wives have stopped going to church because they did not want to answer the embarrassing question, "Where is your husband?" Some wives of prisoners have preferred to lie and tell people that they are "divorced" or that "he died" rather than letting themselves in for the social stigma of admitting that they are married to a criminal.

If a man has been in prison for as little as three years, he has experienced significant emotional trauma, as has his wife. Two emotionally bruised people cannot easily work out their marriage problems alone. In some instances, the church's financial support of professional counseling by a Christian therapist may be just as important a resource as food and clothing.

53

There is really a broader issue here than the marriage alone. The ex-offender's successful transition in the community, the church, and the workplace will necessitate his ability to establish relationships. Because of the shutdown of all emotions during his imprisonment, the typical prisoner will have difficulty with *all* relationships.

For example, the ex-offender may find it difficult to form friendships or make emotional attachments of any kind, and some church members may misinterpret this, assuming the ex-offender is cold or aloof when he actually has a desperate need for friendship.

Alternately, the ex-offender may be unable to judge what kind of attachment is appropriate and what kind is inappropriate. In his desire to make up for lost time, he may force himself on people.

I recall an ex-offender, two months out of prison, who referred to every individual he met as his "best friend." Most of us use the word *friend* sparingly. We have many acquaintances and we are friendly with many people but most of us in a lifetime are fortunate to have one or two very good friends. This ex-offender, who had experienced rejection from his family and had been very lonely in prison, had no models for appropriate levels of attachment. His behavior was based on a wish or a fantasy to be universally accepted. He would lavish people with praise, write them gushing emotional letters, refer to a person who had given him the slightest attention as his "dearest friend in the world!" His words were obvious exaggerations.

Not surprisingly, some people were put off because this ex-offender came on so strong. Unfortunately, in his perception, their response translated to rejection. Anyone who backed off from or failed to return his invitation for an immediate deep relationship became an enemy. Then he would act withdrawn and distant, and other people in the church would be offended by this behavior.

This young man's needs were genuine, but he had little training or experience in getting them met appropriately. His hurry to get on with his life just made matters worse. After all, trust takes time to build. No stranger can force himself on another person, and an ex-offender, in particular, must take time for relationships to grow. This ex-offender was simply moving too fast in the area of relationships.

Depression

Undoubtedly, most ex-offenders will experience significant depression that may be experienced as discouragement, sadness, pessimism, and in the extreme, loss of touch with reality. This depression may be due in part to guilt because they were unable to provide for their families' needs or from a sense of loss when there is no support system after release.

The key here is not to equate depression with a loss of faith. Depression is a natural emotional and physical response to having come through a traumatic event—and incarceration certainly qualifies as traumatic. We may hope that the experience of coming to Christ may avert this despair in the born-again believer, but regenerated ex-offenders may still experience long periods of depression.

Flashbacks

An ex-offender named Ralph was gang raped on his first day in prison. Until that day he had thought of himself as a strong individual, but he was powerless in the hands of a large group of violent men. They beat Ralph physically to subdue him. The rape involved penetration by each of the individuals. Physically he was left bruised and bleeding, but the psychological trauma was far worse because it affected his sense of manhood. The experience left him feeling confused, defiled, and degraded!

The next day, Ralph saw his mother in court. She asked about his cuts and bruises, and he responded with complete denial. He told her he had tripped and fallen down some stairs.

Fifteen years later, long after his release from prison, Ralph was sleeping in bed with his wife. When she turned over and touched him, he screamed and hit her with a closed fist! When he realized where he was, he was remorseful. In his mind, he had returned to the scene of the prison rape.

Ralph had experienced what psychologists refer to as a flashback. This has been well documented among soldiers, who may relive or reexperience the trauma of their war experiences many months or even years after the original experience occurred. Ex-offenders often experience similar flashbacks or disturbing dreams.

Repression

It is not uncommon for people who have undergone traumatic experiences to cope with the pain by completely repressing the experience itself. They may have no conscious memory that the event even happened.

Today we know of many men and women who were victims of incest as children yet remained consciously unaware of the abuse for a significant part of their adult lives. I have a friend whose wife had been sexually abused by her father but was unable to remember until she was thirty-five. She is now in Christian counseling, but coming to grips with such a reality is difficult, slow, and incredibly painful.

The church working with an ex-offender should have a sensitivity to the emotional trauma most prisoners experience. Spouses need a similar sensitivity. They must realize that feelings of panic or irritability are a natural response to prolonged grief and loss. These feelings may not come out the first day or week after release, but they should come out eventually. While it is possible to permanently repress very traumatic experiences, it is usually important that painful circumstances and traumatic memories be faced and healed. The grace of God, a patient family, loving friends, and a good Christian counselor can help the ex-offender find healing and become more emotionally stable.

Suspicion and Paranoia

Many ex-offenders have difficulty trusting, loving, and reaching out to other people. They seem to stay in a mode of constant suspicion that may border on paranoia. It is not wise to walk up quietly behind some recently released inmates and touch them suddenly. They may question the true motives of other people, including the church people who are trying to shepherd and disciple them.

This suspicion may also be a form of anger stemming from bad experiences with authority figures or harsh treatment from other inmates. The ex-offender may even develop a delusion, really a mental disorder, that all authority figures are out to get him. He may also misinterpret the motives and actions of those who are trying to help him.

A couple once invited to their home for dinner an ex-offender who had been out of prison only a week. The wife was concerned about what kind of meal to prepare, and she and her husband discussed the menu for some time. "What if he doesn't like vegetables?" they debated. "Or what if he is a vegetarian?" The concern over what to serve to an ex-offender is a valid one because after release, they tend to avoid at all costs foods that they were served daily in prison, such as beans, rice, scrambled eggs or cornbread.

Finally, the couple hit on what they thought was an excellent solution. They both thought of a restaurant close to their home that served buffet style. Bringing the ex-offender there, they realized, would give him a wide variety of choices and solve their problem.

At the appointed hour, the ex-offender appeared at their door. The couple had their coats on and informed him they were taking him to a place he would surely enjoy. When they arrived at the restaurant, they were handed trays and silverware like the other patrons and invited to go through the buffet line. The newly released ex-offender just stood in line for a long time with a pained expression on his face, clutching his empty tray but not selecting anything. Repeatedly the service person behind the counter asked, "May I help you?" The couple who had invited him just looked puzzled; they did not understand what the problem was. Then suddenly, without warning, the former prisoner hurled his tray into a wall and ran out into the parking lot.

What had happened? The ex-offender had received a very different message than his hosts had intended. He had been in an institution for many years. Standing in line with tray and silverware in hand was just like prison. He had longed to be in someone's home. It did not matter to him what he ate; he was hungry for fellowship and acceptance. When the door opened and he saw his hosts with their coats on, he assumed that they thought he was not good enough to eat with them in their home.

This story illustrates how important honest communication is when helping an ex-offender make the transition back into the free world. If the couple had called the ex-offender and discussed the options with him, he would have surely said, "The food doesn't matter. I'm just looking forward to coming to your home." It also illustrates that prisoners generally leave incarceration with a heavy load of emotional baggage that may cause unpredictable responses. Patience and forgiveness must always be part of the church's response to the newly released ex-offender.

Passive-Aggressive Behavior

Another emotional consequence of incarceration is what psychologists call passive-aggressive behavior. This is a response I have often witnessed. Rather than expressing anger verbally or exploding with rage, the passive-aggressive ex-offender shows anger through a series of small resistant or disobedient actions. I remember one ex-offender I supervised in the Colson scholarship program who acted this way. If I needed a certain form completed, he would keep "forgetting" to fill in the form. In a seminar, if I asked everyone to sit in the first row, he would promptly sit in the last row. None of these acts were particularly serious in themselves, but the overall pattern was clearly passive-aggressive.

Another ex-offender I knew well was always extremely prompt—consistently ten minutes early for every appointment we had. Then one day we had a disagreement, and soon thereafter he began showing up late for our appointments. Sometimes he would keep me waiting for twenty minutes or more, and he would always have an elaborate explanation. The pattern lasted for over a year, until we were able to work out our differences.

Passive-aggressive behavior is typically a tool of those who feel powerless. Prison, of course, is the epitome of powerlessness, and the ex-offender may continue to feel coerced by having to live under the authority of the church, employers, teachers, and so forth. He will be afraid to jeopardize his employment and other relationships, but his anger will come out in passive-aggressive behavior.

After release the ex-offender begins to exercise whatever ways of regaining power that are available. This is something like the two-year-old who has learned the word "no!" Ultimately, the two-year-old is dependent on his parents for just about everything, yet the child begins to discover that he does have some power, although the behavior and the attention he receives is negative.

Personality Disorders and Other Extreme Reactions

For some prisoners, coping with stress has produced harmful psychological changes in their personality. These are commonly called personality disorders—an emotional exaggeration of the functions of a normal personality. There are two personality disorders that present the greatest danger to the local church in terms of games, cons, and manipulations:

- The antisocial, or sociopathic personality, does not feel the pain of other people and even derives excitement from exploiting or hurting people. I will explain in a later chapter how the church can watch out for this personality type.
- The narcissistic personality is extremely self-centered and demanding. He can literally wear out church volunteers and members.

While most forms of emotional fallout can be handled by mature church members who are mentoring and shepherding the released ex-offender , these two personality disorders will require professional help. (I will suggest some guidelines for recognizing these problems in chapter 7).

The church should not be hesitant in recommending Christian counseling from a competent professional psychologist or psychiatrist for an ex-offender when a personality disorder is present. Here are some additional indications that the church should draw on outside resources:

- The ex-offender is increasingly paranoid and can trust no one.
- The ex-offender is having delusions and hallucinations.
- The ex-offender is constantly irritable and at times his anger is explosive.
- The ex-offender is in a prolonged state of depression.

Prayer, of course, is essential when such behaviors exist. Coupled with prayer, however, is the need for professional help.

A Place for Healing

One great flaw in the American criminal justice system,[4] in my opinion, is that it has no place for healing. It is an adversarial system that keeps victims and offenders apart. Prosecutors want victims and their families to hate the offender. Police and politicians label criminals as "the enemy." This works, if the ultimate objective is simply arrest, prosecution, and conviction.

To many, at first glance, this is the way it should be. Prison is a place for punishment, they reason, not for healing. The reality, however, is that 96 percent of all prisoners are eventually released and return to the community. Do we want them to come back with worse attitudes and behaviors? Do we want them to be seething with anger or paralyzed with pain? Without emotional healing, most will not be able to become functioning members of our society.

In April 1992 the television program "20/20" broadcast a feature on Marion Prison in downstate Illinois. I have visited this prison and consider it one of the toughest prisons in America. It has been in lockdown (the prisoners never or very rarely leave their cells) for more than seven years. On the program, one inmate was asked what he thinks about most of the time, and his reply through steely eyes and taut lips: "Revenge!" Without healing, that is the kind of personality that is likely to be loose on our streets. Without a change of heart, these prisoners are dangerous for society after their release.

The church, however, is equipped to play a role that our criminal justice system cannot. The church can bring healing through forgiveness. The church can turn revenge into restoration. And the church can be a vehicle of God's love and caring for the ex-offender who is struggling with the emotional aftermath of incarceration. For every negative emotion, God has provided a remedy.

The greatest and most potent prescription for an ex-offender who is angry is forgiveness. Through the power of the Holy Spirit, the ex-offender receives forgiveness from God, then can seek forgiveness from the people he has hurt, and can finally forgive himself and those who have hurt him.

For the ex-offender experiencing sadness or sorrow, God provides comfort through his Holy Spirit.

For the ex-offender experiencing grief in the death and loss of a loved one, God's Word gives the promise of eternal life.

For the ex-offender experiencing excessive fear the Word gives the assurance that God cares and will protect.

For the ex-offender who is lonely, God provides the strong support group through the local church in addition to family and friends.

For the ex-offender who is jealous, God gives the ability and the power to trust.

Finally, for the ex-offender still experiencing the confusion and the pain of the meaning of his incarceration, God gives the reminder that he is still sovereign and works in all situations to bring good for those who love him (see Rom. 8:28). It is hard to understand how something that feels so bad—like imprisonment—can turn out good. But for those who love and trust God, the hope is in his ultimate plan for our lives, a plan that ultimately works out all things, including incarceration, for good.

Many mature Christian ex-offenders tell me that prison was "the best thing that ever happened to me."[5] These men and women are not in denial, foolishly relabeling the prison experience. What they mean is that God used prison as an instrument for their salvation. God used prison to get their attention. God used prison to remold and reshape their lives toward faithfulness and obedience.

In other words, God has a remedy for every negative emotion, and the local church is the apothecary. This is the place where the ex-offender will get the prescription filled. Love will not drop out of the sky. It will come in the form of the embrace of a Christian brother or sister who has accepted the ex-offender with unconditional love.

A mythical friend will not appear to solve an ex-offender's loneliness. Relationships must build. Trust must be developed. The church body will eventually become the ex-offender's new family.

Anger will not be solved by the ex-offender denying that he feels anger. He will be taught through wise instruction and shepherding to confess sins and to seek forgiveness. And he, in turn, will learn to forgive those who are suspicious or have misjudged or hurt him.

No Time Is Really Lost

It is natural for the ex-offender to desire to make up for lost time. Because he is lonely, he would like instant friendships, but friendships take time and patience to cultivate. A church mentor can help him to be patient.

The ex-offender would like his marriage to function perfectly from day one of his release, but a good marriage takes constant communication, attention, and work. He will need to be patient since both partners are bruised with emotional wounds. A mentor can encourage him to hang in there and, if necessary, to seek counseling.

Because of his romanticized expectations, he would like to return to a society and a church where everyone is friendly and everyone accepts him. But that is a fantasy. Many, especially the unbelievers in society, will be suspicious because he is an ex-offender. It will take time for him to prove himself through his behavior, even among church people. Some people will always be suspicious and may never be convinced he is genuine. A mentor can help him learn to be patient with such people.

He may want to make up for lost time by seeking recognition. Some ex-offenders have a desire to convince their old enemies or adversaries such as police that they have changed. Or they may even desire to start their own prison ministry or move into church leadership positions. A mentor and a loving church can surround the ex-offender with love and acceptance while protecting him from responsibility he is not yet ready for. (Chapter 5 will look at this subject in more depth.)

Coming back to the free world for an ex-offender is like catching up with a moving train. In some cases the ex-offender becomes a runaway train himself—pushing too hard, demanding too much.

This is where shepherding is so essential. He must be taught to express his emotions appropriately, to be patient and not to force himself on people, to work through relationship issues, and to not seek attention until church leadership feels he is ready.

One cannot rush spiritual growth even with a desire to make up for lost time. In God's sovereignty, no time is really lost. God promises us through his Word, "Though the locusts have eaten the fields, God will replenish the harvest" (Joel 2:25–26).

3

The Old Personality in the New Creature

How Much Has the
Christian Ex-Offender Really Changed?

Three months ago an ex-offender recently out of prison proclaimed to me, "I can never commit another crime!" I appreciated his self-confidence. I fully believed he intended never to return to crime, but I wondered why he was not capable of crime and I was. My point is that while it may not be probable that mature Christians will commit crimes and go to prison, neither is it impossible. And it is far from impossible for an ex-offender to fall back into his or her former ways.

On many occasions I have heard converted ex-offenders refer to themselves as "new creatures." And of course they are, according to 2 Corinthians 5:17: "If anyone is in Christ, he is a new creation; the old has gone, the new has come!" I have no problem with redeemed ex-offenders who proclaim themselves to be "new." I rejoice with them in their newfound faith. But it is the inference often attached to that label that concerns me.

"God has reworked me," one ex-offender stated boldly. "I have conquered the old sinful nature!" I was really envious that he had arrived at a state that I covet. In my journey toward spiritual maturity, I constantly battle with temptation and sin. I wondered, there-

65

fore, how it was that this man's transformation inside a prison made him immune to sin. What led to this perception?

If the ex-offender, as a new creature, in no way resembles the old creature, then has he become perfect? Is the regenerated ex-offender incapable of backsliding, sin, and new crime?

New Doesn't Mean Sinless

Often some ex-offenders and the godly church people who support them imply that the ex-offenders' former negative personality traits are gone, that just because they have accepted Christ, they no longer have tendencies toward certain sin and that they have overcome the negative influences of environment and culture. I believe this is a fundamental misinterpretation and misapplication of 2 Corinthians 5:17.[1]

I have been regenerated in Christ for some twenty years, yet I still struggle with my temper; I must continually be on guard to make sure I express my anger appropriately. As a child, I often watched my father fly into rages. Growing up in an Italian home, I was accustomed to communication that was often emotional and at times explosive, and I learned to communicate that way myself. My tendency toward inappropriate expressions of anger did not vanish when I made a decision for Christ. By God's grace, it has been modified greatly over the years, but it is still there. The influences of my family, culture, and environment are strong.

When 2 Corinthians 5:17 is misinterpreted, novice believers and their churches may assume that Christian ex-offenders no longer resemble their past selves. Certainly, a very deep and fundamental change has taken place in them, but this change in attitude, direction, and values does not guarantee perfection.

The only way that regenerated ex-offenders can be incapable of crime or sin is if they are in a new, glorified, sinless body. Christ has not returned, and this is not the new heaven and the new earth. That means that born-again ex-offenders, like all other members of the body of Christ, continue to be sinners. Yes, they are forgiven by the grace of God. Yes, they have the power of the Holy Spirit to resist and overcome temptation. But this remains a

fallen world, and they, like all other humans, remain fallen creatures. To expect otherwise is to pave the way to disappointment
and disillusionment for ex-offenders, for prison ministry volunteers, and for churches.

Basically, people are in prison because they have been convicted of committing a sin, which according to law is a crime. The
label of *criminal* is apt. If prisoners accept Jesus Christ, they begin
a journey that will change their attitudes and ultimately their
behaviors. They will attempt to avoid violence, stealing, and lying.
They will strive to be at peace with their neighbors, they will seek
to serve others, and they will try to become more and more like
the person of Christ.

But even though these individuals are now Christians, their
outward circumstances have not changed. By the judgment of the
courts, they are still prisoners or ex-offenders on parole. More
important, they still encounter temptations inside and outside of
prison—temptations to fall back into playing games and manipulation, to respond violently to provocation, or to hang out with
the same old crowd that got them into trouble in the first place.
In addition, because they are exposed to many conflicting belief
systems and may not yet be thoroughly grounded in Scripture
and sound doctrine, they can be easily perplexed by conflicting
philosophies.

For all these reasons, following Christ is a daily struggle and a
difficult tension for most prisoners and ex-offenders. Even as they
grow in him, they are likely to struggle with sin and make mistakes. To help them grow, they will need careful shepherding by
the local church; a close mentoring relationship with strong,
mature Christians; and liberal doses of both accountability and
forgiveness.

Two Steps Forward, One Step Back

A true story illustrates this point. A young African-American
man was released from prison. He had been convicted of several
serious crimes, including armed robbery and habitual drug traf-
ficking. But church volunteers had visited him consistently dur-

ing his prison term, and by God's grace he became a Christian in prison. On his release he attended a white suburban church north of Chicago and lived with members of the congregation.

By outward standards this young man was a model of a changed person. He often gave his testimony in church and before outside groups, and he made a conscientious effort to stay away from the "old neighborhood" and his former criminal associates.

But then one day he made a mistake. While driving to work, he failed to notice a stop sign. A nearby police car flashed its red light and sounded its siren. The young ex-offender panicked. Rather than stopping, he hit the accelerator. This action of course compounded the original—and minor—traffic offense. And the situation degenerated from there. The young man subsequently ran a red light and another stop sign. He now was guilty of fleeing and eluding as well. These multiple offenses were a violation of his parole status and eventually sent him back to prison.

I was not surprised by the criminal justice system's response to this young man's new crime. What startled me were the comments of some people in his church. Some were quick to judge, saying, "See, he really wasn't a Christian; he was just faking." Others actually used the 2 Corinthians passage to imply that his conversion wasn't real. "He was not a new creation," they said, "he was still just a criminal. The old things had certainly not passed away." They seemed to think that any mistake, any sin, any crime, on the ex-offender's part suddenly voided his entire Christian journey and authenticity.

I found that sad, because I really believed the young man was making progress. Considering all the stresses and difficulties he faced in making a transition back to the free world in a different culture, and considering the chaotic, violent, and sinful street life he had grown up in, a series of minor traffic offenses and a panicked emotional reaction was really very tame stuff. In no way did these new offenses resemble his violent criminal past. As far as I could see, he had taken two giant steps forward and only one step back.[2]

My challenge to members of this church was to continue to love the young man, to be consistent and affirming. I urged them to visit him, write him, and on his next release to take him back again. I believed this was their only clear choice as followers of Jesus.

A New View, an Old Addiction

Let us turn our attention back to this expectation that the ex-offender would be a "new creation," or as one person suggested, that "the old things" or previous criminal nature should have been firmly relegated to the past.

This brings into focus the interpretation of this passage in 2 Corinthians 5:17. Clearly, to me, this passage was concerned more with perspective and with attitude than with day-to-day behavior. One translation suggests that "the ancient ways," meaning the old ways of looking at the Messiah, are gone.

This was true for the apostle Paul. Paul's old view was that Jesus was a mere man. Paul's new way of looking at Christ, after he encountered him on the road to Damascus, was to see him as the Savior. Paul's conversion was at heart a dramatic change of viewpoint.

That's what happens when any of us are born again in Christ. Our worldview changes; we now regard Christ as the hope for our sinful condition. We once made decisions relying on our own thoughts, feelings, and biological urgings. But now we realize that we can make our decisions in Christ, with the Holy Spirit as advocate and resource.

And yet old habits die hard. Our old viewpoint may be gone, our inner attitude may have changed, but old patterns of behavior remain. If we apply 2 Corinthians 5:17 to the individual ex-offender and have an expectation that he no longer resembles his old self, we are overlooking what my friend Rev. Bob Harvey has called "the pursuing power of sin." We are also ignoring the constant struggle with temptation that all believers battle in our fallen condition.

A sociology professor once referred to this struggle as "the human addiction to sin." I like that word *addicted*. Having been the director of a drug and alcohol abuse program, I know how very difficult it is for individuals to overcome insidious dependency even after they have made the choice to put their old lives behind them. We are all very much addicted to sin, and we all must struggle constantly with temptation and the recurrence of sin in our life. We can expect to make mistakes and to depend on God's forgiveness.

Now, this doesn't mean that what we do doesn't matter or that we are exempt from the consequences of our sin. It certainly doesn't mean that since we can be forgiven we might as well give in to temptation and not worry about right behavior. To the contrary, being a new creation means being on a new road, continuing to grow from "babe in Christ" to mature Christian.

We Are Not Alone

The good news in all this, of course, is that new Christians are not expected to grow alone. Being a "new creation" in Christ means more than just changing our attitudes and perspective; it also means coming to a personal relationship with the One who makes it possible for us to grow. As Christians—ex-offender or average citizen—we are now living in a vital relationship with Christ. It is always God who brings us back to himself, who initiates and gives us the grace and the power to overcome sin.

In Colossians 2:6, Paul uses the analogy of roots drawing nourishment from the soil to emphasize how dependent we are on Christ for help with our daily struggles and for our ultimate salvation: "So then, just as you received Christ Jesus as Lord, continue to live in him, rooted and built up in him, strengthened in the faith as you were taught, and overflowing with thankfulness."

I believe this Scripture also illustrates that the decision to follow Christ is really only the beginning. Christians must make a genuine effort to keep submitting our will to God, to keep growing and learning from the Word and relying on the power of the Holy Spirit.

And we must learn to rely on each other as well. To continue to grow, I believe that believers need ongoing contact with other believers—for fellowship, for encouragement, for accountability. It is for these purposes that Christ established his church and told us to shepherd one another. This is especially important for regenerated unbelievers, who usually struggle with especially powerful temptations and difficulties.

Just As I Am

One important thing to recognize about the process of growing to maturity in Christ is that we do not have to be perfect or sinless in order for God to use us for his purposes. The Scriptures are packed with examples that show how God uses weak, sinful people as conduits of his power. He uses them with their unique multifaceted personalities, diversities, and cultural backgrounds.

As a disciple, Peter was impulsive and impetuous, even violent. He made rash decisions and foolish statements, and when the pressure was on he even denied knowing his Lord. Morally speaking, Peter was little different from many ex-offenders. And yet Jesus used him in a leadership capacity.

Was Peter totally transformed by his relationship with Jesus? Did he have to become a perfect person before he was entrusted with leadership in his church? No, Peter clearly continued in his basic personality tendencies even in the early days of the church. He had disagreements and at times quarreled with others. In fact, the same stubborn, determined, bullheadedness that got Peter in trouble became used by God to grow an infant church.

No doubt these tendencies were modified as Peter grew in Christ. Surely the older, more mature Peter was not as impulsive as the Peter who walked with Jesus. But he was still the same Peter—and that was who God wanted. God did not want a wimp. God did not choose a Peter turned Milquetoast. God used Peter with all his strengths and weaknesses.

Some years ago an ex-offender said to me, "I'd like to be in ministry, but I'm just not good enough." But such self-deprecation can be just as debilitating for ex-offenders and the churches that support them as expecting them to be sinless. Both ex-offenders who think they are not good enough for leadership or those who believe they have arrived at a state of spiritual perfection can just as easily be snared by the evil one. The first may never use their gifts for the kingdom; the others may think themselves invincible and suffer a moral failing.

During the forty-year history of his crusades, Billy Graham has used a particular song when people come forward. "Just As I Am" is a wonderful hymn that declares we do not have to be perfect to follow Christ. God accepts us just as we are, with all our faults and frailties, habits and sins. God can initially use us in a weak state, then he begins reworking and remolding us toward greater degrees of spiritual maturity.

Shaky Faith

Another ex-offender once said to me, "How can I attend Bible college when I have so many doubts?" And yet many great men and women of God have struggled with doubts at various moments in their lives.

John the Baptist, for instance, was a great man who spoke with power and authority and who paved the way for Jesus' coming. Yet at a critical juncture in his ministry, John began to have doubts that Jesus was truly the Messiah.

In Matthew 11 we find John the Baptist in prison, sending his followers to ask Jesus the question, "Are you the one who was to come, or should we expect someone else?" It is a vital question because it will either affirm or deny John's ministry. And Jesus doesn't scoff at John's doubts. Instead, he gently responds by urging the disciples to tell John what they have witnessed—that the blind have been healed, the lame are walking, lepers have been cured, the deaf hear, the dead have been raised, and the good news is being preached to the poor. And then Jesus goes on to affirm John by saying, "Among those born of women there has not risen anyone greater than John the Baptist."

Examples of God using people with shaky faith are numerous in the Scriptures. Abraham doubted he could be a father in his old age, and Sarah, his wife, doubted she could be a mother. Yet God kept his promise to Abraham to make him the founder of a people.

Moses doubted his abilities and even tried to bargain his way out of commitments to God. Moses did not think he was capable of leading the people out of Egypt. And yet God used Moses to engineer the Exodus.

The Israelites doubted and squabbled and lost faith with almost every step of the way in the wilderness. They doubted God's ability to help them when faced with problems or obstacles. Yet God was able to accomplish great things through these people in spite of their wavering faith.

In a way, it is unfortunate that one of Jesus' disciples, Thomas, got stuck with the historical label of "Doubting Thomas." As far as I can tell, he was honestly struggling with believing that Jesus had risen from the dead. He truly wanted to believe, but couldn't. And Jesus honored Thomas's doubt, allowing him to touch his wounds before gently admonishing him to "Stop doubting and believe." And to Thomas's credit, when Thomas had seen this evidence, he at once proclaimed, "My Lord and my God!" (John 20:28).

The doubt that Thomas expressed was not the same as despair. He was still hoping, still looking for evidence, not giving up. And the important fact is that Thomas did not stay in doubt but moved to faith, although faith required more for him than it did for the other disciples.

Signs of Spiritual Growth

We should not doubt God's ability to use the wavering faith of an ex-offender. Why should an ex-offender believe he is not good enough? Why should some in the church expect an ex-offender to turn completely away from sin and crime when we are all sinners saved by God's grace and not by our own efforts? It is and always has been the power of the Holy Spirit that enables growth.

God worked through the imperfect personalities of Peter, Paul, Gideon, and David. God will work through the fragmented personality of the ex-offender, too. The church should not expect a transformed, gleaming, shining new person, but essentially the old person with a new attitude, a new direction, and especially a new resource: God's power.

73

When we get to know each other really well in the church, we see weaknesses as well as strengths. We will at times disappoint one another. We will, at times, let each other down. In this respect, the ex-offender is no different from any other member of our congregation. He will at times fail to keep commitments. He may run stop signs, fail to pay a debt, or hurt someone's feelings through careless words or actions.

Yet, at the same time, the church can expect a regenerated ex-offender to show some signs of growth, especially over the long haul. Hebrews 12:14–16 spells out some of the specific signs of spiritual maturity:

> Make every effort to live in peace with all men and to be holy; without holiness no one will see the Lord. See to it that no one misses the grace of God and that no bitter root grows up to cause trouble and defile many. See that no one is sexually immoral, or is godless like Esau, who for a single meal sold his inheritance rights as the oldest son.

The writer of Hebrews also sets forth some basic guidelines that can be followed as indications that an ex-offender is growing spiritually. I believe these guidelines could be put into the following four categories:

1. The inmate should be making progress in leading a clean life rather than falling into immorality. There may be—and probably will be—slips and mistakes, but an overall pattern of moving away from old, destructive habits and toward honesty, purity, and integrity should be evident.

2. The inmate should be seeking unity versus disunity, especially within the body of Christ. If he is chronically quarrelsome and divisive, that's a sign that something is wrong.

3. The inmate should show signs of living by faith rather than wallowing in doubt. As we have seen, God can certainly use people who have doubts, but he also wants us to grow toward deeper faith. The former prisoner who keeps putting his future goals and success on his own shoulders and relies on fate or luck is probably not growing in the faith he needs so much.

4. The inmate should be more concerned with confessing, repenting of, and making amends for his own sins than with judg-

ing the inadequacies of others and blaming others for what has happened to him. One unmistakable sign of spiritual maturity is taking responsibility for one's own life instead of falling into judgment and blame.

The ultimate way for the church to measure the growth of an ex-offender is by watching his behavior patterns over a period of time. Actions are far better indicators of manipulation, deception, or backsliding than words are. A skillful manipulator will tend to rely on words, accompanied by a charming smile. But we truly only know what branch someone is attached to by the fruit they bear.

Some ex-offenders I have known have adopted infantile behaviors because of a long institutionalization that created a dependency state. These individuals can be selfish and very demanding. Others have become complainers and grumblers because that is a common prison attitude. We can be patient with such behaviors, but Paul says clearly that backstabbing, complaining, selfishness, and bitterness are not godly. More important, these behaviors exhibited over a period of time are indication that the ex-offender is not growing spiritually.

If the ex-offender is not growing, the church should not give up on him. Love that maintains clear standards for behavior is important. We support the person yet confront the sin which has damaging consequences for the individual and the church community. The church has an obligation to call all sinners to repentance and impose discipline when necessary.

Old? New? Or Both?

One last consideration concerning the old personality and the new creature: The ex-offender has a change of attitude and direction. He has made a choice to follow Christ and renounce overt sin. But in every other sense, he is still the same person, with most of his habits, tendencies, and cultural and environmental baggage.

That means, for example, that if a criminal used charm and sales savvy to sell worthless junk bonds, as an ex-offender he may be likely to use the very same qualities to raise money for the church. If an inmate has a short fuse, he is still likely to struggle with anger-related problems as an ex-offender. If he suffered emotional damage either before incarceration or in prison, he may still be suffering from the after-effects.

The ex-offender may not be aware that old habits and tendencies lie behind his behavior as an ex-offender. And not all habits and tendencies are bad in themselves. For instance, to the degree that an ex-offender's sales techniques are not deceptive or manipulative, we may call them a talent. Resourcefulness, singlemindedness, loyalty, perseverance, and passion are all qualities that can be used either for crime or for the kingdom of God. But the church in particular must be careful to help the individual examine his life and his motives, and to help him seek renewal, through confession, for lasting change in negative habits.

The fact that the regenerated ex-offender is still essentially the same person also means that he or she will be vulnerable to the same temptations. Unless churches recognize this fact, they may be setting up well-meaning ex-offenders for failure by putting them in the line of great temptation, especially regarding past tendencies and former sins.

Several years ago, a prison ministry leader appointed a newly released prisoner to be treasurer of a large prison ministry movement. But Jonathan had been put in prison in the first place because he had embezzled most of the funds from the large church he had been pastoring! When I spoke with the ministry leader about the wisdom of this appointment, he told me, "Jonathan is a new man. Allowing him to be treasurer will prove that God's power changed him."

The end of Jonathan's story is both unfortunate and predictable. Jonathan embezzled considerable funds from the prison ministry movement. Other people involved in the ministry were angry, cynical, and certainly would have "tarred and feathered" Jonathan . . . if he had not already left town.

I do not know if Jonathan was a true disciple of Jesus or not, but I do believe that, considering his background, he should never have accepted the treasurer's position—and it should not have been offered to him.

There is surely a way back from crime. And there is no better place for restoration and forgiveness than in the body of Christ.

And God truly does grant believers the power we need to resist temptation. In the words of 1 Corinthians 10:13:

> No temptation is irresistible. You can trust God to keep the temptation from becoming so strong that you can't stand up against it, for he has promised this and will do what he says. He will show you how to escape temptation's power so that you can bear up patiently against it. (LB)

But nowhere does the Bible say that God's people should lack discernment or be foolish! Nowhere does it say that we should test God by deliberately putting ourselves or anyone else in the path of temptation. To the contrary, the Bible strongly emphasizes that Christians should "flee" from various kinds of temptation and pray that we will *not* be tempted (see 1 Cor. 6:18, 10:14; 2 Tim. 2:22; Matt. 26:41). It naturally follows that we should never test God's power to change people by putting an individual directly in the path of a known weakness.

A man or woman who has become a "new creation" in Christ is an individual with a new attitude, a new way of looking at Christ, and a new basis or hope. He has begun the process of growing toward spiritual maturity. But all Christians, as long as they remain on this earth, are vulnerable to temptation. All Christians retain some habits and tendencies of the old personality even as we move toward spiritual maturity. And this is true of ex-offenders as it is of any Christians. We do our ex-offender brothers and sisters a grave disservice if we expect otherwise.

4

Who's in Charge?

Helping Ex-Offenders
Who Have Problems with Authority

Society expects released prisoners to become good citizens. And inclusive in that role is a willingness to submit to lawful authority. Working at a job, getting an education, and living as part of the body of Christ all require coming to terms with authority.

But this is not an easy thing for many ex-offenders. Many prisoners are suspicious of authority in any form and usually contemptuous of government. Most have had problems with teachers and principals, and many dropped out of school by the ninth grade. And by definition, of course, the majority of ex-offenders have problems with legal authority; from their first arrest they have been in adversarial relationships with police officers, judges, probation officers, and prison administrators and guards.

Even after these men and women find Christ and after they are released, these problems with authority are likely to continue. Helping an ex-offender learn to handle authority appropriately—both submitting to other people's authority and asserting their own authority—will be a major challenge to a church involved with aftercare.

The Root of the Problem

How do most people learn about authority in the first place? The answer is obvious—by observing their parents or other caregivers. Parents (or grandparents or foster parents) are the first authority figures most people encounter. The examples and the models we observe growing up shape our attitudes toward authority for years to come.[1]

And this is the root of the problem for many ex-offenders, whose primary experience with their first authority figures was essentially negative.

No parent is perfect, of course, and all parents make mistakes. Some set too many or too few rules. Some make bad judgment calls. Some parents inflict physical and emotional pain on children. And some parents simply are not there.

Faulty Fathers

Most male inmates, for instance, lacked a father figure when they were growing up. Either their father was emotionally distant, or he was missing altogether. And this absence of a male authority figure can have powerful repercussions in a boy's life.

Robert G. Andry, in his book, *Delinquency and Parental Pathology,*[2] comes to the following conclusions:

1. Delinquents identify more with their mothers than with their fathers.
2. Delinquents feel love more from their mothers than their fathers.
3. Delinquent boys think their fathers are especially embarrassed to show love and affection openly.

Most prisoners fit the delinquent profile in youth and have ever-emerging patterns of problems with authority.

According to a survey published in 1991 in the *New York Times* and reported on *ABC News,*[3] 25 percent of all young black males in America (ages twenty-one to twenty-nine) are incarcerated or under some form of custody. Homicide is the leading cause of death for young black males. I am convinced that the absence of a positive authority figure—a father figure—in their lives is a very crucial factor in these sad statistics. The absence of involved fathers helps account for the high crime rate in poor, urban neighborhoods and the high rate of incarceration for one race.

One African-American ex-offender once put it this way to me, "Growing up I had no father. There was no one to tell me what to do. I was on my own. I sought refuge in gangs and in drugs . . . just looking for any structure."

Obviously, one's view of authority can become very distorted and convoluted if the parent-child experience, especially the father-son experience, has been a painful one. That was certainly true for me.

I was twelve years old when a Roman Catholic priest, Father Volker, gave me private religious instruction. The catechism he used talked of "God the Father," and that confused me. My own father was emotionally distant. He was a compulsive gambler, usually off at the horse track or in a back room playing poker. He also had a violent temper. I had often witnessed parental quarreling, shouting, screaming, and profanity. If God was a father, was he a father like that?

My mother would cover for my father. "You know," she would say, "he loves you in his own way; he just can't say it or show it." But statements like that do not hold much weight for a young boy who needs a father. If love is intangible, if it does not take you to a ball game or hug you or say the words, "You're a neat kid" or "I love you," how are you to know? If love does not take the time to discipline you appropriately, how are you to know?

In my situation, I did *not* know. I had many doubts about whether I was personally worthy or deserving of love because of the lack of a father's attention. When I heard the phrase, "God the Father," I could only relate to my own human experience. I immediately thought of God as distant, unpredictable, at times unfair, and sometimes frightening.

Father Volker probably knew nothing about my home situation; that was a closely guarded family secret. Even if he did know, perhaps the good priest assumed I could discern the difference between a loving God and a distant father. But whatever he knew,

81

the good priest failed to teach me that God was a caring and loving father, because I had no model for that kind of father.

When Parental Authority Turns to Abuse

I believe many prisoners carry the pain of being unloved, unsupervised, and abused by their parents. That pain comes out in strange ways and at unpredictable times, and it often takes the form of resisting authority.

Many prisoners have been victims of severe physical abuse from a parent or parent figure—a relative or friend of the family. Both male and female prisoners may have been victims of incest or have been sexually abused by people they know, relatives, or friends of the family.

Adults would naturally be angry about such abuse. Children, however, do not know how to be angry, especially at the parent, so they sometimes develop elaborate defense mechanisms. Sometimes children will blame themselves, or they will create a fantasy world in which everything gets relabeled and the hurt and trauma are buried deep inside. Nevertheless, the child cannot help but be left with a warped view of authority figures.

Of course, children are not the only ones who deny parental abuse. The parents themselves—either the abusive parent or the spouse who let it happen—will often rationalize, relabel, and minimize abusive behavior.

Several years ago, I was conversing with my mother about a painful memory I had of an incident that occurred when I was nine years old. My father had forcefully and angrily ejected my uncle, who had been living with us and to whom I was especially close, from our house. I witnessed an intense emotional scene, with everybody shouting, and that scene became branded in my memory.

When I later mentioned it to mother, however, she said, "I don't know what you are talking about. I don't remember that." I wondered for a moment if it had really happened.

Some months later, I was talking to my uncle by phone and wanted to tell him I loved him. As a typical Italian male, he had a difficult time returning the gesture in spoken words. Then I added, "You know, Uncle, it hurt me when my dad kicked you out of our house." He, too, responded, "I don't remember that." Then he grew silent.

I wondered if I was going crazy. That event was very real and painful to me, and I have no doubt that it happened. My mother's and uncle's denials were frustrating because I simply wanted resolution and healing. But the more I explored this behavior, the more clearly I realized that this was part of a pattern in my family. Any unpleasant events were quickly relabeled or minimized, and the feelings were kept underground.

At age thirteen I was hospitalized with an ulcer, and a perceptive doctor quickly realized that my physical symptoms were related to family problems. This doctor confronted my father with the reality of his perpetual absence from the home and his obsessive gambling. He even asked my father point-blank, in my presence, "When are you going to be a father to your son? Who do you love more, horses or him?"

My father probably felt cornered, and he reacted explosively. "Horses!" he blurted out. And on the days and weeks that followed, my father never once put his arm around my shoulder and said, "I didn't really mean that" or "Of course I love you."

My mother, trying to be helpful, would say, "He didn't really mean it" or "It isn't as bad as it sounds." Perhaps if I asked her today, she might even say, "It didn't happen at all."

Emotional and physical pain are difficult enough to deal with, and the practice of denial and relabeling make the hurt harder to deal with by driving it underground. As a result, adults hurt as children carry a lot of negative emotional baggage with them into their marriages, their parenting, and their church life.

I am convinced that a disproportionate number of people who end up in prison suffered emotional or physical parental abuse or neglect. Often denial—their own or someone else's—has robbed them of the opportunity to confront parents, to forgive them, and to begin the process of healing.

Backward Values

In today's real world, there are no *Ozzie and Harriet* or *Father Knows Best* parents. Yet even though all parents have imperfections, the type of poor parental authority most prisoners experienced is extreme by comparison to what most evangelical families have.

Most of the students I work with at Wheaton College come from good families. The students as a whole are respectful, well-mannered, considerate, and ethical; they also embrace biblical principles. These are not inborn attitudes and traits. While it is true that some of our values come from school, church, and government, our value system predominantly comes from our family.[4]

For many prisoners, this principle works in reverse. Their distorted value system also began in their families of origin. Take the case of Ralph, a teenager with whom I once worked. Ralph had been caught shoplifting, arrested, and locked in juvenile detention, and he seemed genuinely confused by this turn of events. Ralph knew right from wrong in the sense of what the law dictated, but I do not believe he understood the spirit of the law; he just could not seem to grasp why he was being punished.

In the months following Ralph's detention, both of his brothers were also arrested and jailed for shoplifting. And I was puzzled, because as far as I could see their home life was not that bad. They had no father, yet their mother seemed a pleasant and conscientious person, concerned about her boys. Why were they all "going bad"?

It was a dilemma I was not to unravel for two years. During that period, I moved from the juvenile to the adult division, and one of my first cases was the boys' mother, who had been arrested for shoplifting. When I summoned her "rap sheet" (list of prior convictions) on the computer screen, I found it was nearly seven pages long!

A month later I discovered in a psychological evaluation of the mother that she had actually conducted a *school for shoplifters* in her home. From the time the boys were toddlers, she would set up a card table in her living room and teach them how to pass the table, lift sample merchandise, and conceal it.

Consider the devastating impact of that mother's conduct on her children. To young children, parents seem almost godlike. These are the people who care for and nurture them, the people who by word and example teach them wrong from right. But what happens when the parents' values are warped?

84

In this instance, the mother taught the small children that it was *good* to steal for the family, and she rewarded them for their skill at theft. Is it any wonder that her thirteen-year-old saw nothing wrong with his actions? Shoplifting and theft had become part of his value system.

Part of the mission for the church working with released prisoners, therefore, is to restructure their value system, to replant biblical values in place of the negative values the individuals learned or acquired.

Negative Messages

Sometimes parents send negative messages to their children. I once heard prison evangelist Bill Glass speak to a group of more than 375 prisoners assembled in a prison yard in New Jersey. "How many of you ever had a mother or a father who predicted you would be here someday?" he asked. To my surprise, almost every hand went up.

Many mothers and fathers have said to their children, "You were born to raise hell!" "Someday you'll end up in prison!" "You'll never amount to anything!" or "You're no good!" And so often these messages have become self-fulfilling prophecies.

I am convinced that the power of God can break that cycle. I do not believe someone who is abused as a child is fated to abuse his or her own child. Certainly the grace of God is more powerful than past experience. But it does stand to reason that patterns tend to repeat themselves unless there is dramatic intervention. Statistically speaking, 40 to 60 percent of all abusive parents were abused themselves.

Awkward Reactions to Hurt

Often criminals will lash out at society or hurt strangers to get back at what their parents did to them. Such behavior is usually the result of unconscious feelings.

I remember a young delinquent who was continually stealing automobiles. After stealing more than forty cars, he was brought before the juvenile court and threatened with a long period of incarceration. But the child never kept a car for more than five minutes or drove it for more than two blocks. He did not want the car. He did not want to deprive the vehicle's owners, who were total strangers to him, of their means of transportation.

The psychologist working with the young man explained to me the motivation behind his behavior. The boy had frequently been witness to domestic violence in his home. His father would beat his mother and was having an affair with another woman. The marriage was quickly dissolving, moving toward divorce. The child in simplistic fashion was trying to focus all the attention on himself. His irrational expectation was that his parents would be compelled to come to court together and would thereafter make up and "live happily ever after."

Adults will recognize this bizarre attempt at family reunification as both unrealistic and fanciful. But the youth's resources were limited. His dilemma propelled him toward some action, and he did the only thing he could think to do.

Some criminals who as children were treated as objects and repeatedly abused begin to dehumanize their own victims. Don Holt, a former Colson Scholar, committed a series of armed robberies in his former life. He confesses, "I never saw my victims as real people." But something changed inside the day that Don forced a white-haired woman onto the floor of a grocery store at gunpoint. The woman reminded Don of his mother. "It was the first time I ever saw a victim as a person," Don said. That realization startled him, and God began to work in his heart.

Or take the case of Peter, another young boy I worked with. He had committed a number of acts of vandalism—spraying graffiti on walls, damaging school property. His crimes were not terribly serious or violent, but he was becoming a nuisance to the community.

Peter's parents had divorced when he was young, and his mother and father hated each other. His father, who had remarried and fathered several other children, never visited or communicated with the boy. And Peter's mother was a chronic alcoholic who was very dependent on her son.

The day-to-day pattern of Peter's life rarely varied. His mother would be unconscious by six in the evening and would frequently urinate in her clothes and vomit on herself. Fourteen-year-old Peter would clean her up and put her to bed. When conscious, his mother would say, "I don't care where you go or what time you come in." The complete absence of structure communicated to Peter, "I don't care about you. I don't love you enough to set limits."

To compound Peter's problems, his father had become a successful businessman after the divorce. Peter's stepsiblings had nice clothes, many possessions, and numerous vacations to exciting places. But Peter lived with his mother in abject poverty, totally ignored by his wealthy father.

As I worked with Peter, I quickly became aware that his crimes were not aimed at getting attention so much as getting back at his father. When Peter would be arrested, his father would be subpoenaed to appear in the courtroom. The father would show up, of course, and would give Peter either minimal attention or a stern lecture. He would not demonstrate affection or show concern for his son. Peter's anger and hatred for his father grew steadily.

Craving structure in his life, Peter actually liked being confined in an institution because the schedule was predictable. He would get three meals a day. The staff showed him attention and concern.

One day I was returning to my office at the juvenile facility and found Peter sitting on the front steps.

"Are you waiting for a ride?" I inquired.

"No," he responded.

"I thought you were released. Why aren't you at home?" I questioned further.

"I want to stay here. I don't want to go back home!" Peter replied with emotion.

"The only way you can be locked up is to commit a new crime," I blurted too quickly, not realizing I had given Peter a plan.

Sure enough, within two hours of his release, Peter had hotwired and stolen a car. Then he called the police himself from a telephone booth. He got his wish and was returned to the lockup facility.

In 1990, while visiting a prison, I met Peter again. "What have you been doing since I last saw you?" I asked the now twenty-five-year-old prisoner. Peter responded, "I've been in and out of prison all this time." Then he added, "I'm getting back at my father!"

Retribution was Peter's fantasy. He thought he was punishing his father with his ongoing life of crime. But in reality, as I pointed out to him, he was his own victim. He was the one who had been institutionalized for more than ten years while his father continued to enjoy the pleasures of an upwardly mobile life.

I have conversations with hundreds of prisoners across the country. I believe many of their crimes are feeble attempts to get back at their parents. Their anger at mother and father gradually extends to all authority figures.

Criminal Behavior and Broken Homes

I don't wish to imply that all children who come from broken homes or lack a father are fated to commit crimes or go to prison. Actually, the effect of family structure on delinquency and criminal behavior has long been the subject of controversy, and studies in this area are inconclusive. Nevertheless, both sociological studies and my own experience point toward certain conclusions.

There is little doubt that the structure of the average American family has changed dramatically over the past fifty years. The "traditional" nuclear-family pattern consisting of a working father, a homemaker mother, and their children is becoming increasingly rare. In its place we see more and more dual-career families, "blended" families, and especially single-parent families. A soaring divorce rate has resulted in a growing number of so-called "broken homes."

Several years ago researchers surveyed Cabrini Green, a very large housing project in Chicago's inner city. The purpose of the survey was to determine how many intact families existed in that housing project, whose occupants were predominantly African-American. The conclusion was alarming. Only 12 percent of the thousands of people who lived in those projects had complete families—a father, a mother, with their own children.

I have not reviewed research that definitively proves a broken home will lead to delinquency, nor does my own experience tell me this is an unbreakable pattern. Many children whose homes don't follow the traditional pattern turn out quite well, especially when they have the advantage of loving grandparents, other extended family, or a loving church family. For me, the key issue is not so much whether the nuclear family is intact, but how much love and structure the children experience. Nevertheless, I think it is fair to say (and I think many single parents, stepparents, and other caregivers would agree) that the breakdown in the traditional family structure has made it more difficult for parents and other caregivers to provide that kind of structured, loving environment for children.

One more observation on the relationship between family structure and delinquency (and subsequent problems with authority): I have known a good number of juvenile delinquents who came from good, loving—and intact—families. I have locked up a good share of delinquents who were the children of college professors, pastors, and even a prominent police chief. But in the majority of these homes a crucial ingredient was missing: The child was rarely disciplined and had few limits placed on him. There was typically little or no supervision at home, and the parents rarely monitored the child's friends. The Bible makes it clear that children need discipline. Without it, the child feels insecure or even unloved and also develops a very inconsistent view of authority.

Misused Authority in the Criminal Justice System

One of the reasons many ex-offenders have difficulty with authority is that they have never known or experienced an authority figure in their life who was not out to get them. We can naturally expect someone to be paranoid about authority figures if he or she has never experienced a loving, kind, and benevolent parental figure or school or church authority.

Unfortunately, many prisoners have also experienced misused authority on the part of those who are sworn to uphold the civil authority of the law. The kind of discipline a criminal receives in America is neither swift nor certain. Since sentences vary from state to state, the justice system does not seem just. Prisoners do not automatically learn respect for proper authority in the criminal justice system. Their conception of an authority figure is someone who means to harm them, limit their freedom, or abuse them.

89

My personal research over my years of being involved with law enforcement has convinced me that many prisoners have experienced injustice from authority figures. They have heard police distort and even lie in the courtroom. They have been brutalized by police officers and guards who take advantage of their power.

The Rodney King trial in Los Angeles in 1992 and the videotape seen on national television only confirms the unfortunate reality that some police do misuse their authority and power. Though two of the officers were convicted, the subsequent criminal acquittal demonstrated that juries and courts are often not sensitive to the depth of the problem.

I often talk to people on urban streets, and they tell me that the only thing unusual about the Rodney King incident was that it was videotaped. Such events rarely get public attention, but they are a common occurrence on many of our streets and in our prisons.

Gordon McLean, a leader with Youth Guidance (a division of Youth for Christ) has worked with gangs for many years in Chicago. He has described numerous cases in which Chicago police officers would pick up kids who wore colors that associated them with a particular gang, drop them off in the rival gang's territory, and announce their presence over the police loudspeaker. This would almost certainly result in a brutal beating for the young gang member. At other times police have worked over or beat up juveniles without just cause.

There are good police officers, of course. Many of them are my friends. As an active member of the Fraternal Order of Police, I socialized with officers for many years, and a police officer was in my wedding party also. My point here is that it is difficult for an ex-offender to immediately respect and respond to authority if he has encountered authority figures who have abused power.

On this point, the church must help guide the ex-offender who has had negative experiences with authority. The goal is respect for all legitimate authority, from community institutions to church leadership to local civil authority.

This respect will probably be most difficult for the ex-offender regarding local police. Many ex-offenders who have been out of prison for many years tell me they still have a strong emotional reaction to seeing a uniform and a badge. Even the sight of a fire-man or a security guard can be unsettling.

Most of us get stomach butterflies if a police car is following us down the highway—especially if we have been going over the speed limit. But imagine how the ex-offender must feel. He has seen more than the red lights flashing and has heard more than the police car's siren. Perhaps he remembers being chased by a similar squad car—or being handcuffed and locked in the back of one. He prob-ably remembers hearing his Miranda rights read to him.

Unfortunately, he may also remember being beaten or other-wise abused by those in positions of authority who misuse their power.

Many ex-offenders can be helped in overcoming these feelings by getting to know Christian police officers, even as members of their church. When they come to realize that there are many good police who embrace good values and love the Lord, they begin to respect their authority without irrational fear.

In the prisons, as well as on the streets, there are good author-ity figures and bad ones. There are Christian guards who help pris-oners and treat them with respect.[5] But there are also guards who turn the other way and pretend not to notice when a prisoner is being abused. Some officials can be bought; they receive money from families to smuggle in drugs. In some prisons, a man who wears a uniform and a badge may physically abuse prisoners indis-criminately.

It does not happen everywhere. Not every prisoner has expe-rienced such abuse. But I believe that the abuse of authority in our criminal justice system contributes significantly to the prob-lems many prisoners have with authority.

Helping Prisoners Who Have Problems with Authority

A prisoner who has grown up with faulty models for author-ity and has experienced repeated abuse from those who had legal authority over him is likely to emerge from prison with a deep-seated anger toward authority figures as well as a lack of understanding of what is appropriate in terms of healthy authority. These problems may assert themselves through many kinds of behavior.

Sometimes the anger will be overt; the ex-offender will respond in rage to anyone who "tells me what to do." Other times it may be quite subtle, even passive-aggressive. An ex-offender may repeatedly fail to fill out a required form; he may show up late for appointments or miss appointments entirely; or he may continually challenge the teachings of a professor or the orders of a boss. If he is interested in ministry, he may want to go out on his own rather than submit to the oversight of a church or a supervisor.

A prisoner who has problems with authority may also have difficulty in situations where he must assert authority. For instance, if he was abused or neglected as a child, he may have a tendency to do the same to his own children. He may play power games at home—either falling into domineering behavior or shirking his responsibilities.

In addition, a prisoner who has problems with authority figures may have some problems relating to God as well. These may be directly related to his early experiences. For instance, if the ex-offender's father was abusive or neglectful, he may have real trouble relating to "God the Father." Or he may find himself resisting God in some areas because the thought of obedience makes him uncomfortable.

It is the responsibility of church leadership to help all people, ex-offenders included, to a maturity in faith. In part, this means helping ex-offenders learn appropriate respect for authority—submitting graciously to legitimate authority and exerting authority appropriately and maturely. An ex-offender's ability to lead a lawful life is to a large degree dependent on the church leaders' ability to do this.

How can the church help an ex-offender who is displaying problems with authority? Because problems with authority are usually based on an experience with misused authority, often in childhood, helping an ex-offender adjust to legitimate authority will usually mean helping him experience it in a healthy way. In a sense, the process is a bit like what psychologists call "reparenting"—a matter of substituting a healthy model for an unhealthy one. Essentially, it involves:

- helping ex-offenders understand the rightful uses and purposes of authority
- holding them accountable for an appropriate response to authority
- helping them exert authority appropriate in their own lives and churches
- modeling the Father's love and acceptance

The Rightful Use of Authority

By definition, authority is the right to command or to enforce laws. Every society that is not in chaos has a structure of authority both public and private. Authority resides in government officials, law-enforcement representatives, employers, church leadership.

The root word of authority comes from the Latin *auctoritas*, which comes from the word *auctor*, the Latin word for creator. It is interesting to note, therefore, that even the word *authority* is rooted in the idea of God as the originator and Creator of the universe. That is the correct definition of authority from a biblical perspective.

Ultimately all legitimate authority is given to us by God. Hebrews 13:17 says,

> Obey your leaders and submit to their authority. They keep watch over you as men who must give an account. Obey them so that their work will be a joy, not a burden, for that would be of no advantage to you.

When an ex-offender rebels against authority, therefore, he is really questioning the structure and hierarchy that God has established.

But there are some conditions for submitting to authority, however: it must be legitimate, it must be legal, and it must be reasonable. A reasonable law reflects a consensus of community values, respects basic human rights and constitutional freedoms. It must also not contradict the laws of our Higher Authority—that is, God. If those standards are met, then we are obligated, according to Scripture, to respect authority and to obey the prescriptions and the limits it sets.

Civil and criminal law is an extension of God's established order. But not every law enacted by government has to be found in the Bible. This means that the Christian cannot indiscriminately refuse to pay taxes, obey traffic signs, or purchase a license plate for an automobile. (It would be a misinterpretation for someone to refrain from stealing, yet fail to obtain a vehicle tag if required by a local municipality.) And yet the Ten Commandments do cover most of the laws that society considers major crimes or felonies, including murder, perjury, and theft.

Part of the church's role in helping the ex-offender be a good citizen and live in harmony within a community is to teach respect for authority and the obligation to obey the laws of the community.

What about laws that are wrong or unfair—that violate an individual's moral consciousness or that perpetuate racism? In most cases, it is best to submit to the authority of the law while working through the proper channels to change the law—voting, lobbying, writing Congressmen and Senators. However, I do believe there is a place for resisting laws on the basis of conscience; this kind of resistance is called civil disobedience.

Jesus modeled this kind of resistance to authority when he cleansed the temple. Jesus committed criminal damage to property when he turned over tables and stalls. He committed assault and battery if he struck any of the money changers or if they were in fear of being hit. Jesus was certainly guilty of disturbing the peace by the commotion of his upheaval. But Jesus had a higher purpose. The law ordinarily says not to take the law into our own hands, but Jesus was also God and the money changers were defiling his Father's temple.

In the 1960s, civil disobedience combined with nonviolent resistance was widely publicized as part of the civil rights movement; blacks quietly ignored segregation laws and suffered the consequences as a way of publicizing the unfairness of those laws. Today,

94

the issue of abortion has pushed many Christians into acts of civil disobedience.

A Christian ex-offender may be arrested for blocking the driveway of an abortion clinic. If he does so with the conviction of heart and conscience that abortion is morally wrong, then his act of civil disobedience, in my estimation, is a risk he takes for the sake of the gospel.

I would add, however, that the ex-offender who participates in civil disobedience should be wisely counseled by his local church to seek an alternative method of protest! He may paint the placards that others will march with. He may write letters to members of Congress.

The arrested ex-offender stands to lose more. The average church member arrested for trespassing while protesting an abortion clinic will receive a relatively light sentence—perhaps a fine or several days in jail. The ex-offender on parole can go back to prison when police discover his or her criminal history. It is in no one's best interest, either the local church's or the ex-offender's, to arouse undue suspicion from the local police or violate parole status, even for a worthy cause.

Holding Ex-Offenders Accountable

In addition to helping ex-offenders understand the scriptural view of appropriate authority, I believe it is important for the church to model appropriate use of authority to the ex-offender. This means holding him accountable for following rules, obeying laws, and respecting those who are in authority over him. In a sense, this is almost a matter of "reparenting" the ex-offender.

If a particular ex-offender in the local church is resisting authority, the church needs to respond appropriately. When the inappropriate behavior is relatively minor, I think it is wise to be patient and loving, earning the right to be heard. We have to let trust develop and build our credibility through meaningful relationship. For an ex-offender who has never had an appropriate model or an authority not out to harm him, this may be a long and difficult process.

At the same time, when the rebellious behaviors are more serious, I advocate confronting the ex-offender in love and even disciplining him when appropriate. Often we confuse discipline with hurting people. (This misinterpretation is often used by people who abuse authority.) But the real root of *discipline* is found in "to disciple," which is to show people the right way. (That is why we call Jesus' followers disciples.) In the biblical model, discipline and love are coupled together.

An ex-offender should be disciplined the same as any church member who is unwilling to conform to Christ-like behavior. One of the best ways of discipling an ex-offender will be to let him suffer the consequences of his own action. Though we are loved and forgiven, God allows us to live through the consequences of our sin so that we might grow in our faith and recognize the foolishness of going our own way. Even if the ex-offender commits another crime, the best response of the church will be to continue to support him through visits and letters, but to let him suffer the consequences of that action.

Disciplining an ex-offender may also take the form of saying no to his requests—for handouts, for inappropriate help, for positions of leadership for which he is not yet ready. In Matthew 7:9–11, Jesus asks the question, "Would a father give his child a poisonous snake if he asked for bread?" (my paraphrase). The answer is an obvious no. A church leader acting in the place of parental authority in the life of an ex-offender must realize that sometimes an ex-offender is asking for snakes when he desires something that involves pride, ambition, worldly success, money, or fame. As human conduits of the Father's love, we must not give our spiritual children snakes. We must know what is ultimately good and dangerous for them.

Our model for healthy discipline is that of God, our loving Father, who allows his children to experience adversity, both to perfect our character and to discipline us. This is illustrated in Hebrews 12:7–11:

> Endure hardship as discipline; God is treating you as sons. For what son is not disciplined by his father? If you are not disciplined (and everyone undergoes discipline), then you are illegitimate children and not true sons. Moreover, we have all had human fathers who disciplined us and we respected them for it. How much more should we submit

to the Father of our spirits and live! Our fathers disciplined us for a little while as they thought best; but God disciplines us for our good, that we may share in his holiness. No discipline seems pleasant at the time, but painful. Later on, however, it produces a harvest of righteousness and peace for those who have been trained by it.

Helping Ex-Offenders Exert Authority Appropriately

David Spong, whose J.O.Y. Ministries is aimed at healing prisoner marriages, points out that many ex-offenders who have trouble submitting to authority often have trouble exerting it appropriately as well.

At home, for instance, "many guys getting out want to reclaim their authority in the home, and that causes troubles." David has seen this happen repeatedly. An ex-offender may even use the Bible to support his claim to be head of the household. He wants to regain his rightful place. He wants to make all the decisions and call all the shots for his wife and his children—and this can cause significant conflict. After all, for better or for worse, the family has managed to survive without him—and it was his behaviors and bad decisions that got him into prison to begin with. "It may not be easy for a wife immediately to relinquish all her authority as soon as her husband gets out of prison and claims leadership," relates David's wife Judy.

In addition, an ex-offender who was abused and neglected as a child will be especially vulnerable to doing the same thing to his own children. Christian ex-offenders are not always good parents. I have known Christian ex-offenders who can preach a dynamic sermon but fail to pay child support. I have known some who are great Bible leaders but do not write or call children they have fathered. Unfortunately, Christian ex-offenders are also not immune to physically or emotionally abusing their kids.

Whether we want to or not, most of us are strongly compelled to parent the way we were parented, and in cases where parental authority has been abused a vicious cycle can be perpetuated. To make matters worse, an offender who is a new Christian may fall in the trap of justifying abuse with Scriptures about "discipline."

Churches can really assist at this point with gentle guidance, continual accountability, and pastoral counseling. The ex-offender needs careful guidance as he learns to win his family's trust and gradually reassert his authority in the family appropriately.

Another area where prisoners may have trouble finding their appropriate level and expression of authority—and where they are especially in need of guidance and accountability—is in the area of ministry and church leadership. I have become more and more convinced that one of the reasons many Christian ex-offenders want to work in ministry but are not willing to join an existing ministry is the desire to avoid and circumnavigate authority. Some have great difficulty in working for others, in following orders, and in being accountable. Most difficult is the ex-offender who wants to become an itinerant evangelist immediately after release. He is not under the shepherding of a local pastor because of his constant traveling. He is not accountable to a specific board. As a result, he is not required to grow into a balanced view of his own authority or anyone else's.

For these reasons, I don't believe that an ex-offender just coming out of prison should start his own ministry until he has had years of adjustment and has proven himself working responsibly under someone else's authority. And I believe the same is true of ex-offenders who desire leadership positions in the church. It is important that leaders pay their dues, especially their spiritual dues, to ensure that they have come to terms with authority issues and are ready to take responsibility for those they are leading. The ex-offender who is a relatively new Christian must be protected and shielded from positions of authority, not thrust into power.

Modeling the Father's Love

One of the most important jobs of the church in helping ex-offenders come to terms with authority is to serve as models of our heavenly Father's persistent, powerful, and unconditional love. This is especially vital for ex-offenders whose own fathers were missing or abusive.

It is vital that churches keep in mind that people who have not been loved can easily come to perceive themselves as not lovable. An underlying sense of distrust, usually accompanied by a poor self-image, acts as a barrier to growing close to another person. For this reason, it is very important for the church to keep reaffirming the ex-offender. If he stumbles, if he sins, if he rebels against authority, we should confront him, we should discipline him, but we must never reject him as a child of God.

Some ex-offenders have trouble comprehending this distinction. After all, when they did bad things as children, they as well as their behaviors were rejected. In the church, we must do the very best we can not to send that message. We must do our best not to confuse an ex-offender's actions and behaviors with his basic dignity as a person. There is no structure on earth better equipped and prepared to express unconditional love than the church. It is difficult for some people to accept unconditional love—but that's no reason not to extend it.

I have met a few ex-offenders who seem determined to set themselves up for failure. They keep pushing limits to see if people will continue to love them or reject them. Their behavior reminds me of two children who quarrel on a sandlot. One draws a line in the sand and dares the other to step over it. When he steps over that line, of course, the first child draws another line, and so it goes.

I once knew an ex-offender who from time to time would push me to reject him. He would say openly, "I don't like you." He would insult me, and he would criticize things I had said or written. Finally, after more than a year of this behavior, I told him, "If you think you are going to do something to get me to reject you, it's not going to work."

He seemed shocked. I do not believe he was even conscious of what he was doing.

As I got to know this ex-offender better over the years, I came to realize that he was carrying many emotional wounds. I represented an authority figure, perhaps even a father figure in his life. Perhaps, on a subconscious level, he was trying to get back at his father by insulting me. If I had reacted to his needling with an emotional explosion or just given up on trying to reach this man (a response he would have easily heard in some circles), I would have confirmed his negative feelings about authority figures, heightened his sense of rejection, and slowed the process of healing. He

99

might have responded with something like, "See, you really don't care about me" or "You don't really trust ex-offenders." Instead, because I was able to confront him honestly but not reject him, we were gradually able to build a relationship.

The parable of the Prodigal Son, found in Luke 15:11–31, is a superb model of how the local church can "reparent" the ex-offender who has shown himself to be rebellious or resistant to authority. This is a familiar parable to most Christians, but I want to retrace the key elements of the story:

First, the son leaves the security of his father's house out of rebellion and out of selfish desire. He no longer wants to live under his father's authority.

Second, after he has wasted his money and reveled with prostitutes, the son is reduced to feeding pigs and eventually becomes so hungry he eats their food. To the Jews who first heard this story, this little detail had vivid relevance. According to Jewish law (see Deuteronomy 14:8), pigs were unclean animals that were not even to be touched. The fact that the son was eating pigs' food showed just how low he had sunk; he had literally hit bottom. This is an apt comparison for many who end up in prison. But God frequently gets the attention of individuals precisely when they have hit bottom.

Next, the son comes to his senses, just as many prisoners do who make a decision to follow Christ, to change their attitude, and to change their behaviors.

Now, watch closely the reaction of the father. The Living Bible paraphrase puts it this way:

> So he returned home to his father. And while he was still a long distance away, his father saw him coming, and was filled with loving pity and ran and embraced him and kissed him. (Luke 15:20 LB)

The son at once admits his sin, humbles himself, and says that he is not worthy even to return. And the father, at this point, does not lecture him. He does not say, "I told you so!" He does not lock the son in a room to meditate on his sins. Especially, the father does not try to make the son feel worse than he already feels. No, the father has an instantaneous reaction of celebration and joy:

Quick! Bring the finest robe in the house and put it on him. And a jeweled ring for his finger; and shoes! And kill the calf we have in the fattening pen. We must celebrate with a feast, for this son of mine was dead and has returned to life. He was lost and is found. (Luke 15:22–23 LB)

This parable is a model for the church in responding to prisoners who have rebelled against authority but then repented of their sins and turned once again to God. Sadly, this is not always how it happens. There have been many illustrations of church people being unwilling to forget and to forgive, especially after an ex-offender has ongoing difficulties in submitting to rightful authority.

But Jesus is making a strong point here. And he makes an even stronger one in describing the reaction of the prodigal son's resentful older brother—the one who had stayed at home and obeyed his father and who complained because *he* didn't get a robe and a ring and a party. Jesus specifically compared the older brother to the Pharisees, who were resentful that sinners were able to enter the kingdom of God according to Christ's teachings, but the story also points clearly toward those of us in the church who resent the fact that ex-offenders can be welcomed back into the church even after they have struggled repeatedly with authority issues.

One final message regarding authority that is especially appropriate for ex-offenders is that even though God's love is often compared to that of a parent, our Father's love is nothing like the limited love of a natural father. Natural fathers make mistakes. They hurt, they neglect, they abuse. The American male as a father often has difficulty expressing love and showing affection to a son or daughter. But God isn't like that at all, and that's the message we must communicate to ex-offenders who have been wounded by inappropriate uses of authority. The message we must get across through our words and through our actions is that God must be obeyed, but God can also be trusted, and God is love!

In the words of Psalm 27:10,

Though my father and mother forsake me,
the LORD will receive me.

5

Hungry for the Spotlight

Meeting a Need
without Making Things Worse

It is not unusual for ex-offenders to seek a spotlight, which is another way of saying they crave attention and affirmation. This craving for attention can easily become exaggerated, obsessive, and ultimately inconsistent with spiritual growth. Unfortunately, in Christian offenders the need for attention can translate into beginning some form of ministry—usually some form of speaking ministry in which they travel from church to church giving their testimony or go into prisons themselves. After many years of work with prison ministries, I have become wary of such spotlight seeking. It is a tendency the church that is involved with aftercare should be wary of as well.

No One to Care, No Place to Go

It is really not difficult to understand why a prisoner who has been incarcerated for many years would crave attention when released. Almost by definition, the experience of incarceration is one of isolation and rejection by society and by friends.

Life on Mars

Many prisoners, especially those serving their second or third terms in prisons hundreds of miles from their hometowns, have had few visits during their imprisonment. Families eventually tire of the habitual pattern of crimes and incarceration and may eventually stop calling or writing. In California, 30 percent of more than a hundred thousand prisoners have never had a visit, and 12 percent have no contact at all with the outside world.

How does that make prisoners feel? Like they are on Mars! In fact, prison could just as well be another planet. Prison has its own distinct subculture, its own rules and power structure. No wonder its inhabitants feel like aliens, cut off from the outside.

There is significant "dead time" in prison. Prisoners have many idle hours on their hands, and they sleep a lot. Even if prisoners are given work to do, it is often meaningless, futile, and does not prepare inmates for a future job.

I once visited a prison for men who were serving life sentences without the possibility of parole. It was the Halloween season, and paper skeletons hung on walls, staring at me out of empty eye sockets as I passed. I soon noticed that most of the prisoners had the same lifeless stare in their eyes. It was as if each cell was a coffin and they were the living dead. I still meet prisoners like that from time to time—prisoners who look like zombies. Their hearts are beating, they are breathing, they are walking, but something is vitally missing inside. They lack the vitality that comes from being befriended and loved. More important, they are missing the peace with God that comes through a spiritual relationship.

I once met an ex-offender who had forgotten his birth date. How can that be? Most of us are reminded of our birthday by friends and family. The people who love us celebrate the fact that we are among them. But during the twenty years that man had been in prison, he had not had a single card, letter, or visit the entire time. He, too, must have felt dead. Forgotten.

This story has a happy ending. A local businessman learned his story from a correctional officer. He found out his birthday and sent him a birthday card. That was the beginning of a relationship that blossomed over several years. The businessman made frequent visits. And eventually the prisoner accepted Christ because he saw Christ alive in the man who had became his friend. When released, the ex-offender went into full-time ministry and today is working effectively with juvenile delinquents. And it all started with a birthday card.

Sadly, however, this happy ending is an exception, not the rule at most prisons. More often, prisoners serve out their sentences in a world that most citizens don't even think about or want to be reminded of.

Release Doesn't Change Things

Countless prisoners and ex-offenders have told me that while incarcerated they live in an almost constant state of paranoia.[1] (The catch phrase is "watching your back," and it's not just a figure of speech!) Also, as we have seen, prisoners live in acute anticipation of their release; that is how they cope with the day-to-day tension. And most of them come to perceive release from prison as the solution to all their problems.

But what is the reality of the typical prisoner's release? There is usually no one at the gate waiting for him. The prison may give him money for a bus ticket, but after that he is on his own. If he has not been fortunate enough to have the support of Christian volunteers and a local church, he literally has a ticket to nowhere.

I was visiting a prison in New Jersey in 1987. As I drove up to the front entrance, a light snow began falling. A young African-American was standing outside the front gate shivering (he had no overcoat). Instinctively, I knew that the young man had just been released. He was holding a small shoebox tied with a string; it probably contained all the possessions he had entered the prison with.

I asked, "May I give you a ride?" He looked at me, perplexed. After a pause he responded, "To where?"

I thought to myself, "What a silly response. If he doesn't know where he's going, how would I?"

Again I tried to be helpful: "May I drive you to the bus station?"

Again, he had the same confused look on his face. "Which bus would I take?" he questioned.

The reality of his situation finally registered with me. This man literally had no place to go. I talked with him for several minutes but needed to be on time for an important appointment with the warden. I was able to inform the chaplain who arranged for a volunteer to bring him to a Salvation Army shelter. But I discovered the release of inmates without direction or a support system was a daily occurrence.

Most state systems are kind enough to point the way to the local bus station and pay for a ticket, but if you do not have a home to go to, if you do not have a support system or any friends, where do you go?

Most states give a released prisoner a check for a hundred dollars. But how do most people cash a check? You or I would go to a currency exchange or a bank, endorse the check, show some form of identification (usually a driver's license), and receive the cash. But someone fresh out of prison probably has no driver's license, no I.D. Chances are he can't even cash his check. Sound like a setup for failure? It is!

Even if the released prisoner manages to cash his check, how long can he last on a hundred dollars? In today's society, he will barely survive for a week in a cheap hotel room.

But isn't a week long enough to get a job—any job? Consider walking into a Burger King or McDonald's and applying for a job. You are required to fill out an application, and part of that form will ask about your job history. At the bottom of the application there may be a question about whether you were ever convicted of a felony.

At the very outset, then, the newly released prisoner is faced with a dilemma. Does he lie in order to get the job? Does he fake a job history? Or does he simply admit that he has been in prison for the last few years, knowing he has probably hurt his chances of landing the job? In order to survive, he may have to resort to playing games.

I remember once talking to a soon-to-be released prisoner (not a Christian). He told me, "They're going to give me a hundred dollars. You know what I'm going to do with it?"

"No," I responded.

"I'm going to invest it," he informed me. "I'm going to buy me a gun!"

At first his response shocked me. But then I realized this man knew far more about street life and criminal activity than he did about getting a job without an education or an employment history. Armed robbery might not be an effective survival skill; after all, it had gotten him into jail in the first place. But it was probably the best survival skill he had, and he was making plans to use it.

Human Garbage

Humans need attention and affirmation. And most of us get that need filled through a vast network of business acquaintances, neighborhood and church friends, and family. Sometimes we take for granted the support system that is there for us, but we still depend on it.

That's not true for many prisoners. Instead of being supported by a network of friends and family, they are more typically rejected. Many words attach themselves to most criminals and prisoners: *reject, loser, scum, outcast.* In many ways the criminal is at the bottom of the social ladder, today's leper. Politicians talk about getting tough on crime. And when it comes to giving attention to a social problem, potholes are more important than prisoners. Local schools and hospitals are more important than ex-offender halfway houses.

Security is not the primary reason we tend to build prisons far from major cities. Most correctional systems do a good job of keeping the outside perimeter of a prison secure. But we put prisons far away because we do not want to be reminded that criminals exist. In some ways, we want them simply to disappear from our communities: "Out of sight, out of mind."

I was once involved with a case in which a fifteen-year-old robbed a woman's apartment. He took $17 in cash and did some minor damage. And the victim would call me every day, requesting that the boy be "sent away." She wanted him to go to "some kind of juvenile prison." She did not care where it was. She did not care how harsh it was.

This boy had no father, an alcoholic mother, and emotional problems of his own. He also had significant learning disabilities. Sending him to a juvenile prison would not have solved his problem. About all it would have accomplished would have been to give him further training in criminal activity. But the woman didn't care. She just wanted him gone! She wanted him to disappear from the community.

What Is Appropriate Attention?

Consider all these factors together:

- social isolation
- lack of possibilities
- rejection by family and friends
- a sense of being rejected by society

Is it any wonder that an ex-offender craves attention? A hunger for social acceptance is understandable. A need to boost self-esteem is predictable. But for churches that are trying to build an ex-offender's self-image, the question is: Is the kind of attention we give the ex-offender appropriate?

In order to monitor what is appropriate, the ex-offender will need a mentoring relationship. He will need spiritual shepherding. He may need counseling for both himself and his family. Financial support may be necessary while he finds a job and tries to get on his feet. And he will certainly need friends and an attentive support system.

But what the typical Christian ex-offender doesn't need—especially in the first year or two following his release—is a place in the spotlight or a leadership position in the church. He almost certainly doesn't need to start his own ministry.

Too Much Too Soon

Unfortunately, many Christian organizations treat ex-offenders in a way that encourages them to seek the spotlight and take on leadership prematurely. For many years I have observed the public parading of atheists, militants, and notorious criminals who accept Christ. Sometimes ministers give the information to the secular press. Ministries use banner headlines in their newsletters.

These "transformed" people appear on Christian television and speak in some of America's largest pulpits.

In some instances, unfortunately, the converted ex-offender then backslides and renounces the faith entirely! What has happened in these instances? Usually the church or ministry was eager to show the world the power of God to change people. But in the process they took a new Christian and put him on a pedestal before he was ready.

The Scriptures specifically instruct us not to take new Christians and elevate them to church leadership. This comes from the qualifications for elder and deacon we find in 1 Timothy 3:6. But we can also apply this Scripture to the tendency to "show off" the new Christian, especially if he had a spectacular, public, sinful past.

Let me be clear. I know many ex-offenders who speak in local churches and do a wonderful job. It is entirely biblical to testify to the power of God working in us. We are all to be living testimonies to God's grace, and this may include giving our spoken testimony in public. But the important question here is one of moderation. There is a significant difference between giving a testimony in one's own church and actually going on a speaking tour and promoting oneself.

The first thing a Christian ex-offender released from prison needs to do is become involved in a local church where he can be taught, held accountable, ministered to, and subject to authority and shepherding. I cannot imagine anything more potentially harmful than for a new Christian, fresh out of prison, to travel from state to state or even church to church, and have no one get to know him beyond the day's speaking engagement.

Another vital step for a Christian ex-offender is to become a tax-paying, working citizen as soon as possible. That means getting a job—and I do not believe giving one's testimony from church to church is really a job. Speaking, if done moderately, is a wonderful opportunity to give God glory. But the tendency I have observed is for the ex-offender to receive a stipend for going from church to church sharing a testimony. I believe that such a practice is detrimental to ex-offenders.

The practice of financially "supporting" ex-offenders is well-meaning. Church congregations are appreciative of those who share their testimonies, and they may be emotionally moved by the story of a dramatic conversion. They will gladly donate money to support an ex-offender who says he needs gas money to get to the next town or money for food and lodging.

But if these churches would think deeply, they might discover that they are helping contribute to the rootlessness of a man or woman who desperately needs stability. They are encouraging the ex-offender to spend time traveling and speaking that probably would be better spent adjusting to normal life on the outside, studying Scripture, and growing spiritually through participation in the local church. In addition, they may be supporting a "ministry" that doesn't really minister. I have known ex-offenders who make a living going from church to church giving their testimony but who really are not involved in prison ministry. They do not visit prisoners. They do not preach the gospel in prisons. They do not coordinate the work of volunteers in a specific institution because they do not stay in any one geographical location long enough to build up an actual ministry.

My caution to the church is this: Before inviting an ex-offender to give his personal testimony at your Wednesday or Sunday evening service, find out what else he is doing. If he is attending school, that is fine. If he lives in the community and is working hard, that is good. But if you get a sense that he is moving from city to city or even around the country, it is reasonable to ask what his ministry is or what his long-term goals are. I am confident there are some ex-offenders whose long-term goals are to continue giving their testimony in different churches for the rest of their life. I challenge the authenticity of that activity as a biblical calling.

Little White Testimonies

Another problem with the practice of "traveling testimonies" is that it easily becomes a way of escaping accountability. An ex-prisoner who gives a testimony in his own church has many witnesses who know him and will be alert to exaggerations and half-truths. An ex-prisoner who travels alone and far will be faced with great temptations to conform his message to his audience. When no one church knows what was said in another church three hundred miles away, the temptation to fall into game-playing can be almost overwhelming.

One day I was attending a prison ministry conference with John O'Grady, the former president of Prison Fellowship USA. An ex-offender presented his personal testimony to a largely charismatic audience. Suddenly the speaker hesitated, looked at his watch dramatically, and whispered, "This is the very day and the very hour that Christ appeared to me in my cell!" The audience screamed "Hallelujah!" and burst into applause. They gave him a standing ovation. John and I looked at each other, amazed at the dramatic coincidence.

Several months later, John and I were sitting together again, this time at a prayer breakfast held in conjunction with an American Correctional Association meeting. The speaker was the same ex-offender we had heard months earlier, and he gave his testimony in almost exactly the same words—almost as if he were reading from a TelePrompTer. Then he dramatically looked at his watch, and you can guess what he said next. John and I looked at each other with a combination of frustration and disappointment.

We chose not to confront the ex-offender. If we had, I am sure he would have had a rationalization—something like, "Christ did in fact appear to me in my cell. I don't remember the exact day or time, but it doesn't really matter, and you see how it makes the audience respond."

Unfortunately, this is not an isolated example, although it is an extreme one. I have heard many ex-offenders who in their testimonies use phrases that seem innocent enough but that actually stretch the truth. They may say, "The other day a man came up to me" when they have actually been using the same illustration for two years—and the particular incident did *not* happen "the other day." That may sound like a small exaggeration, but a story that is embellished easily becomes riddled with exaggerations, and exaggerations soon turn into lies. And this will be an especially dangerous temptation for an ex-prisoner, who until recently has lived in a setting where lies and deception were a primary way of getting attention.

As we have seen, telling "war stories" is one of the major games, and it is a major way of getting attention. A man wanting to seem more important to fellow inmates (or perhaps to protect himself by impressing them with his toughness) will tell elaborate tales about the number of people he has killed or stabbed—even if he has done nothing more than write bad checks. Unfortunately, this game of exaggeration, pretense, and lies can carry over after conversion and after release. After all, the ex-offender still desires attention, and the habit of playing games with the truth can be deeply ingrained. We don't do ex-offenders any favors by condoning such game-playing after their release, even if the lies seem harmless in themselves.

Glorifying the Past

A common motivation for ex-offenders seeking a spotlight is the desire to convert a negative past reality into a present, positive one.

Without debate, being labeled criminal in today's society is a heavy burden—and certain crimes carry a heavier stigma than others. A child molester, for instance, is stigmatized even in prison. In the strange pecking order of prison hierarchy, child molesters are at the very bottom, subject to repeated abuse and violence. And of course, the stigma of this particular crime continues on the outside. I know many Christians who would not even consider relating to or hugging a child molester.

But child molestation is not the only crime to carry a heavy stigma in certain circles. Murder has a stigma all its own, especially if a criminal has killed a police officer. And rape bears a heavy stigma because it is both a sexual and a violent crime.

The bottom line is that all prisoners are social outcasts. Being honest about their background can easily keep them from getting a job. And even in the church, which may be genuinely joyful over the ex-offender's conversion, he may also encounter suspicion and even rejection.

Some ex-offenders relabel their entire prison experience and turn it into something good. This is a game—and one motive is profit.

The apostle Paul writes in Romans 8:28 that all things work for good to those that love God, but he was not implying that bad things actually become good. Rather, Paul is saying that God sees the bigger picture. He can turn our rebellion and the adversity and problems of our life into something useful, something that fulfills his purpose. But what is bad remains bad.

It is never proper, therefore, for an ex-offender to boast about crime. I believe it is inappropriate for an ex-offender giving a testimony to spend twenty minutes talking about sins, crimes, and brutality, and then take ten minutes to explain how God has given him a new attitude.

Part of the desire to seek a spotlight is the desire to turn an embarrassing past into something good before an accepting audience of church people. There is nothing wrong with printing one's personal testimony in a pamphlet or tract, but once again, guidance will be needed to maintain balance.

I am especially concerned when an ex-offender begins to use his story for profit. In my position as director of the Institute for Prison Ministries, I receive many unsolicited manuscripts. Large numbers of ex-offenders have written books about their lives, and many of these are dramatic and moving stories. And from time to time, of course, the testimonies of ex-offenders like Harold Morris, author of *Twice Pardoned,* are of great benefit to the church.

However, not everyone has the ability to communicate in writing, and Christian publishers cannot possibly publish every ex-offender's testimony. I can see how very disappointed many ex-offenders are when they cannot find a publisher for their story, and this concerns me. It is as if their testimony has no authenticity unless it becomes a book. And I have to believe that part of their disappointment comes from wanting the spotlight of being published.

One prison ministry publishes ex-offenders' testimonies. In my professional opinion, they have done a disservice to both prisoners and ex-offenders. Many prisons across the country feature racks of small paperbacks with catchy titles and sensational stories about prisoners who have found the Lord. What troubles me about some of these books is the messages they send to ordinary prisoners.

I have seen books that promote the stories of:

- a mobster hit man who found Christ
- a bank robber who had known Bonnie and Clyde and later was saved
- an out-of-control cop who became a serial murderer and then an evangelist

One ex-offender author wrote about his Vietnam experiences and frequently speaks in prisons. He is a decent man, but since he really does not come under the authority of any prison ministry, he is pretty much a lone ranger going into prisons. He autographs his books like a celebrity.

I once had an opportunity to hear this man speak. The content of his message was largely war stories. The tales of his Vietnam experiences, for instance, were literal war stories. I realized he was illustrating a point. He was trying to emphasize just how bad he was and to explain how God changed him. But he was talking to a group of prisoners, some with violent pasts, about how he killed enemies with his bare hands, cut out their tongues, and ate the tongues! Did violent prisoners need to hear violent stories? I don't think so.

He also included no small amount of political rhetoric and denounced government policies. His audience was made up of men who had problems with authority. His criticism of government policy merely served to feed their discontent and rebellion.

This man was well intentioned. But was his approach helpful or harmful? My concern was this: His trust in the power of God and his proclamation of the gospel was tacked on to the end of a long diatribe of war stories that tended to glorify violence. Books like that, which focus on the sensational past of an ex-offender, send a hidden and negative message to most prisoners.

One prison ministry leader produces video documentaries in prisons. With his camera and portable lights he will venture into cell blocks in search of famous criminals who have supposedly been changed through God's power. Often he focuses on members of the infamous Charles Manson "family," like Tex Watson and Susan Atkins, who murdered a house full of people in 1969. If Manson himself accepted Christ, this individual would probably immediately take his camera into prison and interview him. If John Wayne Gacy or Jeffrey Dahmer (both infamous serial killers) accepted Christ, he would likewise publish a book or do a video documentary about them.

One might argue that the church needs to hear about famous conversions. But imagine for a moment that you are an average prisoner in America. With cameras and lights, the entourage passes your cell on the way to the celebrity prisoner. What message does this send you? How important do you feel?

There are over one million prisoners in America, and most are not famous. They are not Charles Mansons. The vast majority of prisoners are young "nobodies" whose arrests for burglary, robbery, and auto theft made no headlines, except perhaps in a local paper. When they were sentenced in open court, no TV lights were glaring. Perhaps two or three family members were present. Perhaps there was no one! And they were certainly not surrounded by a flurry of reporters as they were driven away.

Fifty-two percent of all prisoners are nonviolent offenders, and half of those who go to prison are sentenced for technical violations of their probation and parole conditions—failing to report to their officers, giving misleading information, failing to take a drug test, or leaving the state without permission. Fifty percent of new prisoners have not committed new crimes, but have had their probation or parole revoked. In other words, they are simply resentenced on their original crime.

How many prisoners are serial killers or mass murderers? Fewer than 1 percent. It would be extremely destructive, especially for the small petty offender, to believe "If only I were a serial murderer, I would get more attention!" It is not difficult for offenders to pick up such messages. After all, the prisoners who get the books are the prisoners who have committed sensational crimes.

Lone Ranger Ministries

Quite a few ex-offenders who feel drawn to ministry actually start their own prison ministries immediately after release. This again can be a form of seeking the spotlight. Prisoners watch Christian television and videotapes. They observe many ex-offenders getting out of prison and immediately starting their own operation and suddenly getting major attention. No wonder they want to do it, too. But in my opinion, this is another activity the church should discourage—both for the sake of the ex-offender and for the sake of effective prison ministry.

During the past ten years, the Institute for Prison Ministries[2] has been tracking some five hundred separate prison ministries across the United States. At first, this sounds great—the more ministries, the more prisoners can be reached. However, we need to seriously consider their longevity, their track record, their effectiveness, and their state of organization. In reality, there are really only about ten national prison ministries in America including Prison Fellowship, Good News, Bill Glass, and Salvation Army. Some of these have maintained an effective ministry for fifteen, twenty, or more years. Each of them is distinctive, but all have an effective organizational structure, a sound and ethical leadership, and a committed corps of volunteers. In fact, these ten ministries account for most of the nearly one hundred thousand prison ministry volunteers in America. It would make sense, therefore, for ex-offenders who feel called to prison ministry to link with one of these existing major ministries instead of launching out on their own.

Even after having said this, I might add that I have no problem with an individual who feels "called" to meet a specialized need in prison ministry that is not being met by one of the larger national ministries. But I believe there is a correct way to begin such a ministry. The ex-offender who wants to start a ministry needs a board of directors to which he is accountable and a reference or advisory board of experts in the field who can help churches and pastors become involved in the ministry. There should also be a commitment to fundraising standards advocated by the Evangelical Council for Financial Accountability.

Unfortunately, the vast number of prison ministries currently in existence seem to come and go rather quickly. Even though the Institute for Prison Ministries routinely updates its computer list, an average of 30 percent of all prison ministries either have their phones disconnected or their letters returned "address unknown" within a period of one year.

To help avoid this kind of turnover and to avoid overlap, jail and prison ministries need to network with each other. Each ministry needs to identify what it does best and consider what other ministry would best complement its work.

In general, most jail and prison ministries fit into one of three broad categories: evangelism, discipleship, or aftercare. Within these broad outlines, most jail and prison ministries fall into the more specific categories of visitation, evangelism, Bible studies, discipleship, tutoring, job placement, housing, halfway-house management, local church support, mentoring programs, drug and alcohol treatment or education, and continuing education. Within these categories, ministries may focus on certain populations such as gangs or juvenile delinquents.

In 1986 while attending a prison ministry conference, I attended the television taping of the Jim and Tammy Bakker show. The theme for the program was prison ministry. During the three preceding days, I had opportunity to meet many of the prison ministry delegates attending the conference at Heritage U.S.A. I was impressed by the fact that many lacked formal education and seemed to have a poor grasp of Scripture, yet referred to themselves as "Reverend," having been ordained by a local church.

One ex-offender introduced himself as "Rusty" and told me he had been out of prison for three years. When I asked him what he was doing, he replied, "I have started my own prison ministry." He then pulled out a business card and handed it to me. Not surprisingly, the name of the ministry was Rusty's Prison Ministry. I asked him what his ministry did and immediately realized that it was unfocused and almost helter-skelter.

As the Jim and Tammy Bakker show began that day, the first guest to appear was Rusty. I was surprised. I certainly believe there is a place for unknown ex-offenders on Christian television. But it was clear to me even after a brief meeting that this man had no idea what he was doing! He had no goals or mission statement for his ministry, yet he was getting major national air time. I couldn't see that encouraging him in this enterprise was either helping him mature as a Christian or furthering the cause of prison ministries.

The fact is that sincerity and caring and a desire to help prisoners are simply not enough to run a prison ministry effectively. I once visited a prison ministry in the South. A nice couple who would fit the category of a mom-and-pop operation was administering a prison ministry out of their home. Near their home was a trailer that had essentially become a halfway house for ex-offenders. Further down the road was a small house for teenage unwed mothers. Two phones hung on the kitchen wall. One was a suicide hotline, and the other doubled as their home phone and prison ministry number. (They also ran several other programs from their home.) I will never forget watching this woman fry pork chops on the stove while trying to talk someone out of suicide.

I am not ridiculing this couple. Their hearts were certainly in the right place. But their ministry is a good example of people overextending themselves. For instance, I doubt that they had any specific knowledge or training in suicide intervention. I have served in that role on several occasions as a telephone counselor at the Billy Graham Center. Talking someone out of suicide requires background and training, and it demands concentration and a cool mind. I cannot begin to imagine trying to do it while frying pork chops!

I am sure this couple felt they wanted to help all the hurting people in their community, but there is a very big difference between the needs of teenage unwed mothers and those of older men on parole. Not every need has to be answered by every person!

I always encourage smaller ministries to work with larger ministries. This is not because I think the larger ministries should swallow up the smaller ones, but because I believe all prison ministries should complement and support one another. We need each other, and we need to network because that is the biblical model. We are all part of the body of Christ. Truly a "foot" is no more important than a "hand," nor an "eye" more important than an "ear." But the larger ministries that are supported by churches and that have trained volunteers are simply in a position to accomplish more if they are managed effectively.

As I have explained in the previous chapter, I suspect that many ex-offenders start their own prison ministries as a way to circumnavigate accountability. Many become "lone rangers" because they

really do not want to have a boss; they want to call the shots themselves. Let's face it: starting a new ministry saves many steps for
the newly released. They do not have to fill out a job application,
interview for a job, or undergo periodic performance appraisals.
The ex-offender simply starts his own ministry and asks the church
to support him. Then, if things don't go well with the ministry, the
ex-offender can simply close up shop and move on. But what does
this say to the local community? And what does this say to prisoners in terms of consistency?

Black-Market Ministry and Other Deceptions

Some prison ministries sell their books. I know of a ministry
whose books and Bibles are underwritten by donors, yet the ministry turns around and sells them to chaplains. That is the equivalent of a black-market ministry!

It is important for churches to be alert to the ethics of prison
ministries administrated by ex-offenders, specifically the "lone
rangers." Ethics, after all, are a matter of honesty. All people in
ministry are called to standards of biblical integrity.

I am aware of a prison ministry event that had dubious goals.
I was very hesitant to give the appearance of an endorsement
largely because of their methods.

One of the ministry leaders wrote to the Minneapolis office of
the Billy Graham Evangelistic Association praising Dr. Graham
for a magazine article he had written almost thirty years before
and asking for permission to reprint it. Whomever he talked with
at the Graham office thought it would be a fine idea.

Some time later, I was at a meeting where this leader was
recruiting volunteers. He was in the process of selling each volunteer a packet of "indispensable" books (actually overstock from
a particular ministry). I found it interesting that each volunteer
seemed to "need" a different set of books. Then the leader stood
up and described a particular manual that he said the volunteers
would be required to buy. He announced, "The foreword was written by Dr. Billy Graham for this particular prison ministry." He
gave the audience the impression that Graham had endorsed this

particular ministry, when in fact he had simply reprinted Dr. Graham's old article.

On several occasions, I have found my name in various pamphlets as endorsing a particular prison ministry when I had neither authorized the use of my name nor even spoken the words they quoted. In other instances I have seen copy taken verbatim from Institute for Prison Ministries publications and used in pamphlets without permission. Even our photographs, which are copyrighted, have been reprinted without permission.

Some ex-offenders who have begun their own prison ministries will send unsolicited materials—books, pamphlets, or videos—to a church, then bill them. Of course, they are putting the burden on the church to return the materials. If they are skilled manipulators (and many are) they can communicate their feelings of rejection clearly, playing on the emotions of the church people. Sending materials unsolicited and then trying to get a commission or a handling fee is a con. The church should be wary of such tactics. And ex-offenders need to be held firmly to standards of ethical integrity.

Grandiose Games

Over the years, I have had many ex-offenders come into my office with plans and blueprints for prison ministries. Sometimes they are architectural drawings, sometimes actual blueprints, sometimes just verbal descriptions of the planned ministries. The problem is that the plans are often grandiose and unrealistic.

It is difficult to dispute a man or woman who says, "God has called me to start this ministry" or "build this program." It is hard to argue with a call from God. People hesitate to dispute God or question heavenly apparitions, and that opens the door for games and manipulations.

I do not believe churches must automatically be committed to backing an individual's program on the basis of a vision, dream, or "visitation." Unless several believers have received confirmation from the Holy Spirit, private vision should not carry obligations. We can only know God's will collectively and in time, through prayer and the confirmation of other believers.

Ultimately, grandiose plans are a form of needing a spotlight. One ex-offender who visited my office had blueprints for a large building, a project that would cost millions of dollars to build. Each wing was intended to meet a particular need for a different group. There would be a wing for drug counseling, one for teaching job skills, another for a establishing a transitional living facility.

My counsel to ex-offenders is to start small, prove themselves in small things, and work up progressively. My advice to churches is to be cautious when ex-offenders start playing grandiose games.

Another game some ex-offenders play when they create their own prison ministry is creating what I call the perpetual sense of urgency. If speaking in a church, a ministry leader will say, "Without your help, souls will not be saved this week!" or even "There are ex-offenders who have no home, no food, no family tonight!"

We ought to keep in mind that our taxes go to local social service agencies and shelters that also assist the homeless and the hungry. It is entirely proper for the church to work with existing structures in government. We do not have to do it all ourselves. And we certainly don't need to fall for game-playing on the part of an ex-offender who plays on our sympathies.

Yet another game I have seen involves hints of a revolutionary idea that must be kept a secret. I have had several ex-offenders come to me with the "solution to crime." They have some plan or gimmick that will revolutionize the justice system, stop violence, or cure crime. Any level-headed, intelligent person knows that such grandiose thinking is a nonsolution in and of itself.

What to Look for in a Prison Ministry

I am not saying that ex-offenders should never become involved in prison ministry. In fact, many ex-offender leaders are doing a fantastic job running prison ministries. I think, for instance, of Frank Costantino, who runs two halfway houses in Florida and maintains an excellent relationship with the Florida state government. Sam Huddleston is an ex-offender who does a wonderful job of matching volunteers with prisoners in institutions across California. Jack "Murf the Surf" Murphy, an evangelist who works with Bill Glass, is one of the finest prison evangelists living today. Good News Jail and Prison Ministry, the largest supplier of independent chaplains to jails, thrives under the competent leadership of ex-offender Harry Greene, a man of tremendous integrity. I know many chaplains who are ex-offenders and are doing a mighty work for the Lord. Let's not forget that Charles W. Colson, the founder of America's largest prison ministry, Prison Fellowship, is also an ex-offender. Many of the graduates of the Colson scholarship program at Wheaton College have become strong, ethical leaders in jail and prison ministry.

Not all ex-offenders in prison ministry, in other words, are simply striving for attention or seeking to escape accountability. At the same time, there cannot possibly be five hundred prison ministries in America without many "lone rangers" who have no accountability to anyone. After all, anyone can invent a name and put it on a business card. Anyone can print letterhead on stationery. Part of what a church must do before endorsing a prison ministry, writing it into the mission budget, and having the ex-offender speak in their church, is to thoroughly investigate their mission statement and their track record. There are several areas to examine.

Sound Theology

If the ministry has a newsletter or any descriptive pamphlets, try to get a sense of what their theological position is. You can also find out by asking a chaplain who has observed the prison ministry at work in an institution.

One particular red flag for me is a prison ministry that stresses a specific theological tangent or that emphasizes a particular distinctive. Ministries that do what my good friend Bill Glass calls "majoring in the minors" are less likely to be theologically balanced and could actually do harm.

A very frustrated and confused prisoner once wrote to me about a prison ministry that had visited him. This man had accepted Christ when a local church group visited his prison. He didn't understand the full implications of following Christ, but he knew he needed to change his life. Then, a few weeks later, a different prison ministry came into his institution. One of the counselors saw a pack of cigarettes in the prisoner's shirt pocket and immediately proclaimed, "If you smoke, you are not a Christian!" The man wrote me this poignant question: "I have been smoking for thirty-five years. I know it's a bad habit, and I want to stop. But am I a Christian or not?"

How unfortunate that he even had to ask the question—and how sad that this prison ministry made such a big issue out of his smoking while failing to minister to his larger spiritual needs! Certainly, smoking is not a good habit. But a prisoner has a lot of emotional and psychological baggage to get rid of, and smoking is among the least of these problems. In time God will give him the power to overcome the habit—if he is loved and supported in becoming firmly established in Christ.

Theological tangents merely serve to confuse prisoners. One ministry will come in and say that someone is not a Christian if he was "sprinkled" and not baptized by immersion. Another prison ministry will say, "Unless you have the gift of tongues and the anointing of the Holy Spirit, you are not a true follower of Christ."

I can hardly think of anything more important in preaching and evangelism to prisoners and ex-offenders than to stay with the basics—sharing the good news of what Jesus Christ did to liberate man from sin. Prisoners will have ample time to study the Bible, overcome bad habits, and even argue theology once they basically understand their salvation by faith through Christ.

At the same time, it is very important that the basic theology that is taught should be biblically sound. A church that is considering supporting a particular prison ministry should carefully observe the theological expressions of the ministry to determine if it is teaching biblical truth.

One prison ministry I encountered—one that was supported by local churches—was teaching inmates that all roads lead to heaven. "It's okay to be a Hare Krishna," they said. "It's okay to be a Muslim. There is one God, and he will eventually accept everyone." Which Bible was this prison ministry teaching from? The New Testament says clearly that Jesus is the truth and the way and that there is no other route to the kingdom. Surely the local churches would have stopped funding this ministry if they had known what the ministry was really teaching!

I know another prison ministry that "specializes" in cults. Cults are a problem in prisons, but this particular ministry is obsessed with talking about Satan worship and all the various cultic aberrations instead of preaching the Good News. I have a concern that this consistent emphasis gives too much attention to Satan—even if it's negative attention—and may actually be giving ideas to prisoners who are already predisposed to the power of Satan.

Yet another theological red flag to be considered is the prosperity gospel—the idea that accepting Christ will make all an individual's wishes come true. I believe this false gospel is one of the great theological dangers of modern culture. I have heard individual prison ministries promising through preaching that if they accepted Christ the doors of the prison would swing open. By what authority do they say this? It is a blatant falsehood to promise something like that; a prison ministry has absolutely no control of release dates!

The most common version of the prosperity gospel, of course, implies that following Christ will bring material wealth. I read recently in a newsletter that one prison ministry was putting on a fashion show at Riker's Island, a prison near La Guardia Airport. Female models were coming in with mink coats and expensive jewelry. Obviously the male prisoners were entertained by seeing the lovely women. But the prison ministry rationalized the event by telling the prisoners that if they changed their ways and accepted Christ, their wives would have beautiful minks and jewelry and they would be able to drive flashy cars as this ministry director (an ex-offender) did.

This is not only a corruption of the gospel, but a cruel injustice to the prisoners. If there is anything they do not need, it is the lure of materialism. In fact, the desire to get something without working for it is what sent most people to prison in the first place. Chances are that few male ex-offenders will ever be able to give their wives a mink or expensive jewelry or drive flashy cars—nor should they. That is simply not what the gospel is about.

I suspect that the ministry leader's real motivation, whether conscious or unconscious, was to flaunt his material success to his former peers. At the same time he was sending a very negative message. It is my hope that any pastors reading such a newsletter would have disciplined that ministry leader and stopped funding him.

Consistency and Longevity

Longevity is simply another word for consistency. Churches that are thinking about funding a prison ministry should ask how long the ministry has been in existence. For instance, if I know that a prison ministry has been coming to the same institutions for five years or longer, I have a good indication that its staff and volunteers may have had good days and bad days but are basically committed to their calling.

The reverse is also true. When a ministry goes out of existence after six months or keeps changing location or names, I grow concerned. How can a ministry let families, prisoners, and ex-offenders know that it is available to serve them and then disappear, leaving phones unanswered and mail undelivered?

Some of the major prison ministries in America are excellent examples of longevity in ministry. As I write, Prison Fellowship has been in existence for eighteen years, Match-Two for twenty-three years, the Bill Glass prison ministry for twenty-four years, and Good News Jail and Prison Ministry for twenty-seven. And the corrections work of the Salvation Army goes back more than one hundred years!

A Concern for Unity

A concern for unity is a very important quality to look for in a prison ministry because it shows that the ministry is committed to fundamental biblical standards. A prison ministry that has strong territorial tendencies—that claims a particular institution as its own, holds back from sharing with any other ministry, and constantly criticizes other ministries—is one to be wary of!

From time to time, for instance, I will hear a prison ministry badmouthing Charles W. Colson and Prison Fellowship, the ministry he founded. Colson is a prolific writer, an articulate speaker, and, in the best sense of the word, a celebrity in the evangelical church. A keen student of history and theology, he speaks with a truly prophetic voice in the evangelical church today. I have had the privilege of meeting and talking with this man on numerous occasions and have developed a deep respect for him as a person.

More important, I believe that Colson has made a giant contribution to prison ministry by making it acceptable and respectable to the white middle class. A mere thirty years ago, prison ministry was a second-class citizen. The number of prison ministry volunteers has literally quadrupled in that time, and I attribute this rapid growth to the beginning of Colson's Prison Fellowship ministries. Considering that Prison Fellowship International is chartered in forty-five countries, who can doubt that God has his hand on this ministry?

So why are some ministries negative about Prison Fellowship? Basically, I think they are envious of Colson's celebrity and his ability to attract followers and donations. This is sad. Those of us in prison ministry should be grateful that he has raised the level of professionalism in this ministry. As ministry leader Gordon Mclean says, "You never diminish your own work by supporting someone else's work."

I know one prison ministry leader in particular who staunchly refuses to work with other ministries. His operation has grown relatively large over the years, and yet many other ministries know firsthand that he is divisive. Another prison ministry leader was once having an argument with a colleague. The one leader sought forgiveness, but the other responded in writing by declaring, "I refuse to forgive you!"

I find it hard to believe that God will honor such an attitude. We are to sacrifice our own pride and ego for the sake of the kingdom of God. And that essentially is what it means to have a spirit of unity.

Set Up to Fail

Over the ten years I have observed prison ministry closely, I have seen many ex-offenders fail after being put in leadership positions. In some instances these ex-offenders even fall into self-destructive behavior. While writing this book, I received the news of three ex-offender Christian leaders who committed suicide. These individuals were all charismatic. They were all gifted. They appeared regenerated, living for Christ. They seemed to be doing a good job as leaders.

It would be wrong to pass judgment on the suicide of an ex-offender leader, even though we would like to believe that hope in Christ and the support of a Christian community could more than compensate for clinical depression. In most instances, this is what happens. In those regrettable instances where it doesn't, we can only assume that the inner struggle and turmoil was simply overwhelming for that person. It is appropriate, however, to consider some of the pressures that weigh on an ex-offender in a leadership role and consider some ways those pressures can be relieved or avoided.

Perhaps part of the problem derives from the role of the ministry leader in our society. It is an old but true axiom that "leadership is lonely." The higher one moves up in positions of responsibility, the more authority one acquires over others, and the more one increases in reputation, the more difficult it becomes to reach out to others for help. Why? Because leaders, especially males, are usually taught that asking for help is a sign of weakness, and they believe that leadership and weakness cannot coexist.

This is especially true for the ex-offender. Having overcome a difficult past in which his self-esteem was assaulted by society, the courts, other inmates, and self-recrimination, many ex-offenders feel compelled to adopt the image of the invincible leader. Another reason the ex-offender leader may be reluctant to ask for help is the fear of appearing vulnerable. In prison, vulnerability was equated with weakness—and again, it was assumed that a leader cannot be weak.

Unfortunately, we as a church may help perpetuate this image. We are aware that no human being is perfect. All we need do is look at the first disciples of Jesus to see that he used a group of men who could be petty, quarrelsome, prideful, indecisive, and treacherous. And yet we seem to expect our leaders to be free from such human weakness. We sometimes parade the ex-offender leader as a model of regeneration or a walking "advertisement" for the ministry he represents. Not surprisingly, the ex-offender is likely to have a hard time being honest about his failings and temptations.

As a result, the ex-offender leader often puts more and more energy into appearances. He continues to smile, to speak with authority, to look bold and courageous—the way he thinks a leader should look. But inside the ex-offender leader, as in every other Christian, is weakness, sin, temptations, doubts.

Billy Graham once quoted a clinical psychologist who said that more than half the ministry leaders in America live in fear that they will be "found out." Another way of saying that is although Christian leaders are expected to project the image of being strong, almost to the point of being saintly, they are not immune to the inner turmoil of weakness and sin. And because so much is expected of them, they live in fear of losing everything when people realize they are not all they appear to be. How much more true is this for the ex-offender leader, who has so much to live down!

Here again the church often does not help the ex-offender leader. The numerous speaking engagements, the published testimonies, the Christian radio and TV appearances all send the ex-offender leader a message: "You are a model for others to follow. You are a regenerated person, a true disciple of Jesus, and (subtly) almost a saint." All these statements may indeed be true, but they may also make it harder for the leader to be honest about his all-too-human weaknesses.

Sometimes the urge to make up for lost time propels the ex-offender to seek a leadership role prematurely, and he may succeed because he "appears" ready. But skills that are so evident on the outside, such as the ability to speak or write well, may hide an inner immaturity. The inner person may need time to "catch up," time for inner strengths such as patience and humility to build. The work of grace, on which we all depend, requires time to operate.

Certainly we ought never to elevate anyone—whether ex-offender or not—to a level of leadership without an intricate system of shepherding and mentoring. Leaders in prison ministry, like other ministries, have usually studied under other leaders. But once they achieve a certain level of leadership, there is often no one to "minister to the minister." This tendency is particularly harmful for the ex-offender, who is in special need of the checks and balances, the support system, and the accountability that are so crucial for every Christian.

A Proper Place in the Spotlight

There are many ex-offenders who are leaders in prison ministry today who have tremendous integrity. It was once said that some of the greatest mission workers are the people who were saved through the mission. I think this is true in prison ministry also. Prison ministry leaders who were saved through a prison ministry can be especially effective because they maintain a humble sense of their roots and a deep compassion for people who are walking a path they once walked.

I am not writing, in other words, to deny ex-offenders a proper place in church leadership, an appropriate place in our pulpits, or a fair opportunity to share their testimonies through publication. What I am advocating is a system of accountability, guidance, and spiritual shepherding that will keep ex-offenders from embarking on ego trips or playing games to get attention.

Ex-offenders who are new Christians are spiritual babies who need to be carefully nurtured by the church. They should not be thrust prematurely into positions of high responsibility and visibility; in fact, they should be held back if possible. They certainly should not go on the speaking circuit until they have begun making a real life for themselves and been given the opportunity to develop and demonstrate emotional and spiritual maturity. And they should not be assisted in the process of becoming "celebrities." If that is God's plan, it will happen in God's own time. Spotlight seeking is counterproductive for the church, for the ministry, and especially for the ex-offenders.

6

Finding a Church Home

What Ex-Offenders Expect
(and Get) from the Local Church

Research indicates that more than 80 percent of all ex-offenders never find a home church.[1] Why? There are a million possible reasons. But a good starting point for understanding this reality—and changing it—might be to look at the offenders' experience of church in prison and their expectations of what the church in the free world is like.

A Church Behind the Walls?

Several years ago I produced a training video that featured prisoners' testimonies from the Christian community at Leavenworth Penitentiary in Leavenworth, Kansas. I called the video "The Church Behind the Walls." But when it was released, several chaplains began to correct me in my choice of a title. These chaplains strongly believed that there really is no church within a prison. There is a "gathering of Christians" they said, and there is a chapel. But according to the criteria for a church found in the New Testament, and the cultural evolution of the church in America that include nurturing the whole family, sacraments like marriage, and outreach to foreign missions, what takes place in jails and prisons is not a church.

It is certainly true that the gathering of Christian inmates in a prison is very different from what we would think of as a church in a local city or suburb. And it may be true, as some attest, that the population in jails is too shifting and transient for a true church to develop. It may be true that the leadership structure in a prison gathering does not resemble the "elder system" described in the New Testament church, and that few chaplains are in a position to serve as full-time pastor to their inmate flock. It may also be true that few inmate-leaders meet the qualifications for church leadership described in Titus 1:5–9 (blameless lives, sensible, a reputation for not being wild or disobedient, not violent or dishonest, and so on).

For this reason, it may be more appropriate to label an inmate gathering as a "Christian community" rather than a "church"—although I know some chaplains who would still argue strongly that there are churches in prisons where the inmate population has longer sentences. And of course, all Christian inmates are part of the larger, universal church, the body of all believers. I believe the gathering of believers in prison are by definition a "chapel." But no matter how you label it, this gathering of "two or three" in the Lord's name (see Matt. 18:20) can be a powerful force for good in the lives of the prisoners.

The Christian Inmate's Experience

With that introduction, let us evaluate what life and worship are like for the average Christian inmate. Especially for offenders who are converted in prison, these experiences will largely determine the expectations the prisoner will have on release—and may affect the likelihood that they will become involved in a church after their release.

I have worshipped with prisoners in over one hundred prisons across America. In my observation, they all have certain factors in common.

A Prison Minority

First, in all of these prisons, Christians represent a relatively small percentage of the total prison population. In a prison of two thousand inmates, for instance, it is not uncommon for there to be a core group of seventy Christians. If we evaluate the size by the higher standards of spiritual maturity, that number will decrease. Seventy to one hundred inmates would typically attend a Sunday service in a large institution. Being greatly outnumbered intensifies pressure on these individuals.

A Prison Counterculture

Second, the Christian population in prison has a value system very different from the general population. All the distinctives of a Christian community, including kindness and brotherly love, are considered weaknesses by the dominant prison culture, which reinforces such sinful behavior as lying, manipulation, stealing, and violence.

Tested for Their Faith

Third, not surprisingly, it is not uncommon for the faith of this smaller group to be tested. They may be ridiculed. They may be persecuted. They may, in fact, be physically threatened or even injured for refusing to go along with the gangs, the drugs, the violence, and the dehumanization of other prisoners.

But testing is not a new experience for God's people, nor is it without purpose. For example, Hebrews 11:8–9 plainly shows that Abraham had to sacrifice the security of family ties to follow God. Then in verse 13 we observe that some of the followers of God died without seeing their rewards. Verses 35–40 show that faith tends to reap abuse from the world. The persecution and alienation that some Christian inmates experience is entirely consistent with the Scriptures. But the Scriptures also suggest (Rom. 5:3–4) that adversity can perfect a person's character. And Scripture assures us specifically of God's love and protection in times of persecution. In the words of Psalm 27:1 (LB), "The Lord is my light and my salvation; [He protects me from danger] whom shall I fear?"

All this is to suggest that the Christian ex-offender may in some ways be a stronger Christian than many in our church today. At any rate, the ex-offender who suffers for the sake of his faith is in a very biblical situation.

Demonstrative Worship

Fourth, worship in a prison tends to be demonstrative and charismatic. The liturgical structure is loose, and there is room for spontaneous prayer. The sharing of personal testimonies is usually an important part of the service. Inmates are usually very vocal in their responses, and exclamations such as "Praise the Lord," "Hallelujah," "Praise Jesus!" and "Praise God!" frequently ring out. The prisoners also feel free to kneel and raise their arms. The services generally end with an altar call or an invitation, and the inmates are invited to go forward and make a decision for Christ.

Prison worship services tend to be more emotionally than intellectually based. Generally speaking, the preaching is simplistic, not mentally stimulating. Prison Bible studies may call for more vigorous study, but the services are generally reserved for rejoicing and praising. Baptisms, for example, are occasions of great celebration. In one prison Christian inmates have converted an old tank, once used to wash horses, into a baptistery, and all gather around it in great joy when a fellow believer is baptized.

I find all this understandable and commendable. In dark places like prisons where depression and despair abound, Christians are in special need of heavy doses of praise and emotional support.

The Presence of the Holy Spirit

But this is not to imply that prison services are mere emotional exercises. To the contrary, I have seen abundant evidence of the Holy Spirit's presence and power in prison worship. I have witnessed many prisoners' speaking in tongues with profound interpretation, and I have observed moments of genuine prophecy.

Several years ago, I was invited to speak in a major United States penitentiary. The day before the service, I sat in my hotel room and searched my Bible for Scriptures to use as a text for my talk. Matthew 25:36–39, Hebrews 13:3, and Isaiah 42:7 are commonly quoted in prisons because they speak specifically of visiting prisoners and releasing the captives, but I wanted to give these men something they might not have heard. After nearly four hours of study, I found three Scriptures that I believed would be fresh and meaningful to my audience.

At the service the following day, before it was time for me to speak, a prisoner got up and said, "The Lord laid the following Scripture on my heart." Then he began to share one of the passages I had selected for my message. Then, to my amazement, a second inmate stood up and shared a Scripture he believed the Holy Spirit had given him; it was another one of the texts I had selected. Finally, a third inmate got up and shared the third Scripture I had selected. How could they have possibly known what Scriptures I had planned to use? I had not mentioned them to anyone, not even the chaplain.

After my talk, which was based on the three Scriptures, several prisoners came up to me and congratulated me on my ability to build a message spontaneously around the Scriptures the inmates had given me. I assured the inmates that I had chosen those passages—or the Holy Spirit had given them to me—the day before in my hotel room. I am convinced that "coincidence" was really a confirmation to the inmates, a reminder that "the Lord has not abandoned you. Even in these dark, evil places, God will put his hand upon you and the Holy Spirit will reveal his truth to you!"

Life-Changing Encounters

Because I read letters from many prisoners, I am often able to discern patterns in their experiences. Several years ago I began to notice a common thread that ran through many of their letters. A prisoner would tell of hearing the gospel through the influence of a volunteer, a chaplain, or a religious tract. Then he would describe an experience of actually meeting Jesus in his cell—seeing a vision of Christ—and as a result committing his heart to the Lord.

Are these descriptions of visions just figures of speech? What did these prisoners actually experience? Did they literally meet the Lord in their cells? It's hard to know for sure, especially with the prevalence of exaggerated storytelling in prisons. But the stories were remarkably similar. And because the letters came from all parts of the country, I think it is unlikely these prisoners compared notes or copied each other's experiences or testimonies. And guards, chaplains, volunteers, and others would often confirm that a radical change in the individual's behavior often followed one of these reported encounters. Typically, he would turn away from violence and profanity and become gentle and kind.

Charlie Pratt is an example of a prisoner who was as evil as they come. A former Mafia enforcer, he was a brutal animal in prison, and he had spent twenty years of his life there. No one wanted to mess with him.

Then one day, Charlie claims, he encountered Jesus in his cell. And almost immediately, an amazing change came over this hardened criminal. Charlie had once been labeled as "incurably criminally insane." For years he had been kept on heavy dosages of tranquilizers and undergone extensive psychiatric treatment, which had no effect. But now he was gentle, friendly, rational. The guards and other prisoners couldn't believe the difference, but they couldn't ignore it, either.

Charlie's transformation after that encounter in his cell was both real and long-lasting. Since his release from prison more than fifteen years ago, he has become a prison ministry leader. He has committed no crime, though his past criminality was habitual. He has had no new arrests. He has never had to return to psychiatric drugs or to therapy. If Charlie is faking, he is doing a very good job of it!

I am convinced that something unique and special happened to Charlie. Whatever he experienced in that cell, it was dynamic enough to change the heart of a cold and cruel criminal. And because I know Charlie, I am not inclined to scoff at the similar stories that inmates tell me in their letters.

Is it possible that Christ, through the power of the Holy Spirit, would reveal himself to a prisoner in such a unique way—apart from an evangelist, a chaplain, and religious readings? Most of us in the church would say that is not our experience. But most of us have been nurtured in a church environment or at least a safe environment. I think it is possible that God uses more direct means in more extreme circumstances.

I have never been a prisoner, but I once lived in a cell—a monastic cell in a Benedictine monastery. Only God knows how totally sold out I was to the institution of the church. And then I encountered God. I did not have a vision of Christ, but I had a unique transforming experience in a cornfield late one night. It was enough to make me turn away from years of legalism, clericalism, and institutionalization.

I know in my heart that my experience in the cornfield was real, and that makes it easier for me to believe that many prisoners may indeed have a dynamic personal spiritual experience. From the depths of their brokenheartedness and their suffering, they reach out to the only person who can save them from themselves, their sin, and their situation . . . Jesus Christ. And they find him! Perhaps this is another reason why there is so much rejoicing in prison churches and chapels.

Expectations and Disappointments

Let us now consider the various aspects of the Christian prisoner's experience and consider how that experience shapes his expectations after release.

A Different Approach to Worship

In prison, the inmate's experience of worship and the Christian life basically has had these characteristics:

- The "congregation" is a small Christian community that must exist against persecution and ridicule.
- The worship is often joyous and spontaneous.
- Worship tends to be unstructured, with contemporary music, shouting, and praising.
- Inmates are usually hungry for personal testimonies about the faithfulness of God.
- The worship experience is open to the presence and action of the Spirit.

137

- The spiritual experience of Christian inmates in prison includes an openness to prophecy, visions, a powerful personal experience, and encounter with God.

If this has been a prisoner's experience for several years, what might we logically deduce the ex-offender expects the outside church to be like? And at what points is he likely to be disappointed?

Many ex-offenders tell me that the experience of suburban church worship is "dead." And it is true that our mainline denominations tend to be relatively sedate in worship. Our experience of gratitude and praise may be genuine, but we express it in less overt ways. There is an emphasis on silence and reverence. And while these can be very meaningful elements of worship, the ex-offender may never have experienced this approach.

A set liturgy can also seem very strange to an ex-offender who is accustomed to more spontaneous forms of worship and who may still be chafing from years of being told what to do and when to do it. The experience of liturgical worship, which can be deeply meaningful to many Christians, will likely feel confining and strange to a newly released ex-offender.

The ex-offender can no more expect most churches to make massive liturgical changes than the church can expect the ex-offender to sit quietly, with hands folded, listening to a message while he restrains his voice, his body, and his spontaneity. And this dilemma is one of the primary reasons why ex-offenders do not easily find a church they are comfortable with. The experience of church in a prison is so very different from what most of our churches are like that many inmates quickly become bored, unstimulated, and perhaps unchallenged.

Because of this difference in worship style, the ex-offender who finds himself in a typical mainline Presbyterian, Methodist, or Lutheran church will probably not feel comfortable. A church with a high liturgical structure (like many Episcopal, Roman Catholic, Greek Orthodox, and Anglican churches) may be a real turnoff for the ex-offender unless he has had previous experience with such liturgical structure.

It would seem that a charismatic or Assembly of God church would more closely fit the previous worship experience for many inmates. But the church the ex-offender attends, like most of us, is determined more by geography than by denominational distinctives. Ex-offenders tend to worship where they live, and they tend to go with the friends or the family who have taken them into their homes. If they have a relationship with a volunteer, they will be attracted to the volunteer's church.

The radical difference in worship experiences can lead to a great problem for the ex-offender: a critical spirit. I have discovered many ex-offenders who judge the local church unfairly on the basis of their disappointed expectations about what worship will be like.

I hasten to add that these disappointed ex-offenders are not entirely wrong in their assessment of the church! At least some of their disappointment comes from encountering churches who are not living up to their calling. For instance, many ex-offenders expect the church in the free world to be on fire for evangelism. And unfortunately, evangelism is just not the top priority for many of our churches. Middle-class values tend to label churches as successful if they grow in size and number, keep their budget balanced, and offer a great number of programs for the whole family. Church growth is often defined in terms of new buildings, an expanded parking lot, and increased attendance on Sunday mornings.

Granted, there are many churches both in the inner city and in the suburbs that are actively involved in evangelism. Willow Creek Church in South Barrington, Illinois is a good example, as is the Brooklyn Tabernacle Church in New York. And there are certainly many other examples. Nevertheless, an ex-offender who finds himself in a typical mainline suburban church is likely to be disappointed by a lack of commitment to evangelism.

The Experience of Barriers

Another common area of disappointment for a Christian ex-offender is based on the expectation that churches on the outside will be waiting for him with open arms. But the reality is that most churches do not know where to begin in meeting the unique needs of a man or woman being released from prison. As a result, they often put up barriers that can keep the ex-offender from feeling accepted and welcome. These may not be conscious barriers, but they are real and daunting to the ex-offender.

Much has been written in recent years about the problem of making buildings accessible to physically challenged people. For instance, my good friend Joni Eareckson Tada, who is a quadriplegic, has helped open my own eyes to the architectural barriers many churches present to the physically challenged. "Two or three steps are a formidable barrier to someone who is wheelchair bound," she says.

And Joni also points out that these barriers are very effective in keeping the physically challenged out of certain churches. As she puts it, some pastors and church people will say, "We would love to have disabled people in our church, and if they come, we'll build a ramp." But Joni's point is that wheelchair-bound persons who pass a church and see the architectural barrier never feel a warm invitation. They never get past the initial barrier.

The same is true of the emotional and psychological barriers that often confront the ex-offender in middle-class churches. These barriers may take any of several forms. One of the most obvious is clothing.

Ex-offenders who attend church in a middle- or upper-middle-class neighborhood quickly notice that people are dressed well, at least by their standards. A male ex-offender may not own a suit or even a tie. A female ex-offender may not have a nice dress or even own a dress. Inmates may be wearing the same clothes that were issued to them when they first went to prison but now are hopelessly outdated.

From the very outset, therefore, ex-offenders may feel different and out of place in the typical suburban church. And while in reality, no one may be looking at them or looking down on them, paranoia sets in easily. They may feel that they stick out like sore thumbs because they cannot dress as well as everyone else.

Barriers occur on other levels too. We have already discussed the differences in style of worship that can leave an ex-offender

140

feeling chilled and unwelcome. In addition, many middle-class worship services can leave ex-offenders feeling dumb and out of it! The church filled with college-educated people usually selects a well-educated pastor who can quote the latest books, take a scriptural text apart with contemporary exegesis, and quote Greek and Latin origins. But most ex-offenders are functionally illiterate. Unless they have been tutored or educated while in prison, they are likely to function at about a fourth-grade level. It follows that an ex-offender may easily feel left out in a very intellectually focused group, even when no slight is intended.

Even very basic lifestyle differences can put up barriers that ex-offenders feel keenly. An ex-offender whose marriage is falling apart may feel left out in a family-centered congregation. An ex-offender who is having trouble finding a job may feel out-of-place in a congregation full of doctors and lawyers. The music may be unfamiliar. The furniture may be too formal. Any number of factors can combine to make an ex-offender in a suburban church feel like a fish out of water.

The Deacon's Daughter Syndrome

One of the most painful barriers that too many ex-offenders encounter is what I call the "deacon's daughter syndrome." In other words, we welcome ex-offenders into our churches, but we place limitations on them that we would not put on anyone else. We want the ex-offender in worship. We want him to tithe. But considering his background, we do not want him looking at the deacon's daughter. What this simply means is the ex-offender is welcome as long as he keeps his distance. We may call him a brother in Christ, but we don't want him as a son-in-law!

I can think of a vivid example of this that happened several years ago. A particular woman was active in prison ministry for many years. She traveled to churches speaking about the acceptance of ex-offenders. But then her daughter fell in love with an ex-offender, and this prison ministry leader found it impossible to accept him. She wanted more for her daughter—perhaps a lawyer or a doctor for a husband. I believe she truly felt compassion for ex-offenders and was committed to prison ministry, but now her involvement with prisoners had hit too close to home.

In time, this woman came to accept her new son-in-law. But I think her initial anger and rejection was a testimony that spoke louder than anything she had ever said in her church presentations. Unfortunately, the loudest testimony was a negative one.

Is this not where the "rubber meets the road" after all? If we believe God has changed someone, if we want them to be a vital part of our church and Christian community, can we at the same time close some doors to that person? Are we fearful they might be related to us someday? Would we arbitrarily put a limit on their ability eventually to ascend to church leadership?

Is Separatism the Solution?

All this presents a dilemma. Should all churches operate at a fourth-grade educational level to make ex-offenders feel more comfortable? (Even that would not work for those who cannot read or write at all.) Should middle-class churchgoers constantly "dress down" to make ex-offenders feel at home?

Because of all these differences, some people feel that ex-offenders should have their own churches. One prison ministry leader told me some years ago that he believed only ex-offenders could meet the spiritual needs of other ex-offenders. He called for churches that were totally separate and exclusive. "The pastor should be an ex-offender," he proclaimed, "the choir should all be ex-offenders, and every member should be an ex-offender as well." On the surface, this might seem like the most comfortable solution for the ex-offender, and it might relieve a good number of middle-class churches.

But is such a concept consistent with the New Testament concept of the body of Christ? I do not believe it is. What emerges clearly in the Acts of the Apostles is an intimate community of repentant believers sharing fellowship (koinonia). They formed a community of self-giving love (agape) responding to the needs of their brothers. With no class distinctions, everyone is a servant, empowering the powerless and sacrificing in service. The church needs diversity, black and white, poor and rich, educated and illiterate. We need each other, and we can learn from each other. My fear is that separate ex-offender churches would excuse other churches of the responsibility of ministering to the needs of ex-offenders and their families, and it would rob ex-offenders of access to mature Christians who can serve as shepherds and mentors.

Ex-offenders have many spiritual strengths to share with the larger church. They have had experiences from which we can learn, not to mention their personal testimonies. Many Christian ex-offenders have been brought back from the dead; they are living examples that no one is beyond the power of God. I have often felt that the worse the crime, the more glory God receives when an inmate is born again!

Building a Ramp of Welcome

The problems of bringing ex-offenders into churches on the outside are real and not easily solved. They have to do with social settings, differences in culture, and a diversity of church experiences. They also have to do with very real fears and concern for the safety and well-being of others in the congregation. We are naturally afraid of child molesters, rapists, and murderers. But I know of child molesters, rapists, and murderers who are strong born-again believers. We can only explain such changes because of the grace of God. We should never limit God.

This is not to suggest that there are not reasonable precautions the church should exercise in opening arms to ex-offenders. I have already mentioned some of these precautions, and I will explain them in more detail in coming chapters. At the same time, the church needs to work hard at finding ways to overcome emotional and psychological barriers that keep ex-offenders from attending. We must consciously build the ramp of welcome.

Starting on the Inside

One of the most effective means to the end of bringing ex-offenders into the church is to begin *before* their release, through a strong mentoring program that matches committed volunteers with individual prisoners. Once a relationship is established between the volunteer and the inmate, it becomes natural for that volunteer to invite the prisoner into his or her church after release.

Also, if the members of a certain church are highly visible in the prison—conducting services, giving gifts to the inmates' children at Christmas, and writing them letters of spiritual encouragement, then it would seem natural for the prisoner to feel welcome at that church.

More than one hundred thousand church volunteers are currently involved in sharing Christ with prisoners. Yet prison ministry is largely a phenomenon of the white middle-class church, and in some jails and prisons the minority population exceeds 70 or 80 percent. What are the implications of this imbalance? We know that love, friendship, and caring can transcend many boundaries. But because of the prevalence of con games and manipulation, the average volunteer's ignorance of street life can be an obvious hindrance.

At the Cook County Jail, one of the largest facilities in the country, the majority of the more than eleven thousand inmates are African-American. Most come from very poor homes and the housing projects. Many are school dropouts. Their world is one of high unemployment, gang influence, and casual drug use. Into this jail setting come middle-class white volunteers. They know very little about the urban reality of these prisoners.

I say this to simply suggest that as we cultivate a Christian witness in the prisons, we need wise, well-trained volunteers who are sensitive to cross-cultural issues. We certainly need more Hispanic and African-American prison ministry volunteers as well.

Preparing Inmates for Church Life on the Outside

One important way to solve the problems of disappointed expectations and emotional and psychological barriers is to work at preparing inmates for the experience of church on the outside. Chaplains and volunteers who work with prisoners while they are still confined can help them develop a more realistic picture of a diversified church with a wide variety of liturgical styles and temperaments.

For example, chaplains and volunteers can expose Christian prisoners to a wider diversity of religious experiences. For instance, many prisoners tend to be limited to popular religious books, audiotapes, videos, and television programs. While many of these are good, in my opinion they tend to represent only a narrow subculture within the Christian church, and many are spiritually shallow as well.

For instance, inmates are rarely exposed to the stories and ideas of such Christian giants as John Calvin, Martin Luther, John Wesley, or Jonathan Edwards, or even such modern Christian leaders as C. S. Lewis, Karl Barth, Paul Tillich, or Dietrich Bonhoeffer. And although the history of the church dates back to the time of Christ, inmates are even more seldom exposed to the work and contributions of the early church. Such important figures as Augustine, Thomas Aquinas, Thomas a Kempis, Frances de Sales, and Francis of Assisi are seldom mentioned.

One obvious limitation at this point, of course, is the limited reading ability of most prisoners. But I believe that a chaplain or volunteer can pull out some of the more accessible passages or translate many of these writings into wordings easily understood by most prisoners.

Without this exposure to the great history of the church, the prisoner often gets only a popular, restricted version of Christianity and is ill prepared for the diversity he may encounter outside the prison walls and is limited to a relatively shallow and immature view of what it means to follow Christ.

For instance, many inmates become exposed to various forms of the "prosperity gospel," which can be injurious to any new Christian but especially harmful to an inmate. I have heard volunteers promising prisoners that accepting Christ will open the prison doors to them. That is blatantly dishonest (the volunteer has no influence over this process) and sets the inmate up for acute disappointment. The same goes for promises of material prosperity.

The truth is that following Christ while in prison will probably make conditions worse for the prisoner. Although he will have a newfound sense of peace and joy in Christ, his external conditions may actually get worse because his new value system will clash with the dominant culture. And he certainly will have no guarantee either of a quicker release or of material wealth.

145

In addition to exposing prisoners to more variety and more depth in their reading and ideas, I believe chaplains and volunteers should attempt to provide prisoners with experience in a variety of worship forms. Not only will this prepare them for the many different forms of worship they may encounter on the outside, but different worship experiences can meet needs that are neglected in the typical prison service.

Rarely, for instance, have I been in a prison worship service where a significant period of silence was observed. Churches in the more liturgical traditions such as the Roman Catholic church, the Greek or Russian Orthodox church, and the Anglican church have much to teach us in terms of the value of meditation, silence, and contemplation. Prison is a noisy, chaotic environment. I believe that many prisoners would welcome a worship experience in which time is set aside just to be quiet and listen to the voice of God.

I believe it is also important to teach the prisoner who is a new Christian that following God must not be built on an emotional foundation. If we equate God with feeling high and joyous, what happens when we are blue and lonely or just "blah"? A faith that is dependent on "high" emotions may dissolve away when the emotions are gone.

The experience of the apostle Paul can be instructive in this regard, especially because Paul himself spent significant time in prison. Paul often uses the word *joy* in his letters, even those he wrote from a prison cell. But Paul never confuses joy with happiness. The difference between these two words, in my view, is the difference between religion that is based on emotion and religion that is based on God's truth.

Happiness is transitory; it has to do with conditions that come and go. But the kind of joy Paul was talking about was the deep inner sense of knowing God, sensing the presence of the Holy Spirit, experiencing the peace of God that Billy Graham has talked about for over four decades. When we have that joy, nothing can shake it. When we know that God is truly present in our lives, we can get through the storms and the dark times.

As we lead prisoners to spiritual maturity, we must be careful to keep the realities of life before them. Even though they are Christians, they are still vulnerable to sickness and death. There will be times when friends let them down. They will be disappointed and even betrayed; there may be times when their families—or their churches—may misunderstand or even reject them. But through it all, they can always continue to live and grow in the peace, joy, and love of Jesus Christ.

Tearing Down Barriers

Once the prisoner has been released, there are a number of practical steps churches can take to draw the ex-offenders into their midst and help them feel welcome. One of the most obvious is to work on removing the common barriers that tend to make ex-offenders feel out of place.

The solution to the problem of the inmate's not having proper clothes is a fairly simple one. Since most middle-class Americans own more nice clothes than they could ever hope to wear, people in the church could give an ex-offender some appropriate clothes. Second, to help ex-offenders and others feel more at ease, perhaps we in our churches should dress in more casual attire.

If the church is serious about bringing in ex-offenders, including the poor and the homeless, it would certainly also seek some solutions to the problem of people being excluded by a lack of education. Tutoring and literacy programs coupled with appropriate spiritual education is one way to nurture. One possibility might be to have two services—one for church members who require the challenge that comes with spiritual maturity, and the other for the newer "baby" Christians who require a simpler approach.

The Scriptures speak clearly here. Not everyone is ready for the spiritual meat of the adult banquet table. The author of Hebrews makes a clear point in chapter 5, verses 12–14, that the baby cannot sit down at a banquet table and digest spiritual "meat" while he still requires "milk." We certainly do not nourish and nurture the baby Christian by forcing him to the table.

Meeting Economic Needs

We must also teach our churches that ex-offenders will have unique economic needs. Not only might they need economic assistance to live; they also will probably be unable to support the church financially for some time.

I remember once attending a church budget meeting in which we were talking about adding some parking. I was shocked to find that adding just a few spaces would cost thousands of dollars. In recommending that we go through with the project, the church treasurer, a good man, showed an interesting choice of words: "If the church can attract four giving units, we can pay for the additions to the parking lot."

I turned to him abruptly. "Giving units?" He realized what he had said and turned a little pink. He had of course meant new members of the congregation, but he had fallen into the trap of thinking of church members primarily as sources of revenue.

Churches today, with their large capital expenditures of property, buildings, furniture, and equipment, struggle with many of the same realities that homeowners face: mortgages, utility bills, landscaping, and maintenance. And although we do not bring people into our churches to pay for the upkeep—our desire is to lead them to Jesus Christ—churches do rely on members for financial support. If we are to have meeting places, however, we must teach sound principles of stewardship, giving, and tithing.

But churches simply cannot expect ex-offenders to fit in with the tithing structure immediately. Most ex-offenders are quite poor—at least poor in the material sense. The cost of a legal defense is usually devastating to a family, and then they are deprived of a wage earner as well. They often lose their home, and the wife goes to work for the first time. Some families of inmates have to go on welfare to make ends meet. Some may have moved in with relatives. And the financial picture does not typically change with the inmate's release—at least not right away. The released offender rarely has a job waiting for him or her, and what employment is available rarely pays more than minimum wage.

What this means is that reaching out to an ex-offender and his family will probably mean offering some economic assistance as well. At first this may be a matter of direct economic support; a newly released inmate may need food, furniture, toiletries, clothing, and help with rent, especially before he manages to find a job.

In the long run, however, the most valuable contributions are the skills that will help him help himself.

A Work Ethic

I appreciate an ex-offender who is willing to humble himself and do whatever work is necessary to help his family. This shows a real commitment to taking responsibility for his life. For this reason, the Colson scholarship program at Wheaton College helps put ex-offenders through college but still requires that they pay for a portion of their education themselves. This demonstrates a commitment to their own goals and future.[2]

Several years ago, a man wanted to enter our program with substantial credit card debt and no savings. We realized that since he would not be eligible for loans or other forms of financial assistance, he might easily require the slot of two individuals. We postponed his entrance into the program for one year and told him that during that year he would have time to work and be in a better position to help himself and his family.

The year went by, and he said that he was unable to work. He had done some odd jobs, but basically only his wife was working. This was an able-bodied man who could have worked at a fast-food chain and made some contribution toward his future. I do not know all the reasons that he was unable to do this, but I was convinced that he had demonstrated a basic lack of responsibility. After a full year he had not improved his situation at all.

This is where the church can help. There are business people in every church who could help an ex-offender find employment and assist him with fundamental job skills. Most of us remember the adage, "It is good to give a man a fish. It is better to teach him how to fish!" If every church took in one ex-offender, helped him acquire some practical job skills, then served as a catalyst to getting him employed, I am confident that each of those ex-offenders would succeed and that their self-esteem would increase along with their income.

The ex-offenders I have known over the years do not really want a handout. They want to support their families and prove themselves, but they may need a little help to do this.

One of the ex-offenders in the Colson scholarship program is an excellent example of a man with a strong work ethic. During his four college years, Chuck's wife worked during the day while he went to school full-time. Then he went to work at night—from eleven in the evening to seven in the morning. Chuck Mathis is a man who was willing to make sacrifices in order to help himself. He knew that a college degree would increase his chances for productive leadership and ministry. And he also knew he had a responsibility to his child and wife.

What ex-offenders expect from the local church is often unrealistic, but what ex-offenders receive from the local church is often un-Christian and uncaring. The church must be willing to adapt to the unique needs of the ex-offender. Pastoral counseling may be needed to shore up a shaky marriage. Family members may need winter coats; children may need new shoes.

In order for ex-offenders to thrive and grow in our local churches, we must be patient, generous with our resources, and willing to help them with the most basic skills. Many single ex-offenders are inexperienced in the practical skills we take for granted, including:

- balancing a checkbook
- cooking
- obtaining a driver's license
- filling out a job application
- looking for an apartment
- interpreting a contract or a lease

Church members who have teaching skills can make a huge difference by tutoring ex-offenders and helping them improve their communication skills. This in turn will increase their chances of finding gainful employment or being admitted into a community college or university.

Above all, a strong mentoring relationship and constant shepherding will maximize the growth of the ex-offender in the local church.

7

The Risk of Loving

The Reality of Cons and Manipulation

A volunteer in prison ministry for nearly forty years was once asked, "In working with ex-offenders, aren't you afraid of getting conned?" The volunteer responded, "But I *do* get conned! I do get manipulated from time to time. That is the cost of loving."

The volunteer had an excellent point. All Christians take a certain amount of risk in fulfilling the mandates of the gospel to work for social justice and to reach out to hurting people. The risk may merely be to our comfort level and our resources, but there is also the potential for deep hurts on an emotional level.

That is the risk of following the gospel, the risk of loving. That is certainly the built-in risk of working with ex-offenders. Initially, before there is time to judge authenticity by the fruits of the Spirit and the evidence of regeneration and growth, we necessarily take ex-offenders at their word. And taking people at their word opens the doors to manipulation and cons.

An Easy Mark

A "mark" is the identified victim of a con man.[1] Unfortunately, churches and church members can be easy marks for deceptive ex-offenders. In fact, some manipulative prisoners and ex-offenders have learned to prey on churches in particular.

In many respects, the church can be a more gullible victim than almost any other agency or institution in society. The simple reason is that Christianity is based on hope and optimism. Christians are taught that kindness and generosity are virtues, and Scripture tells us specifically that we are to reach out to others.

Matthew 25:34–46 clearly teaches us that we are to minister to the needy in the same way we would minister to Jesus. Hebrews 13:2 tells us that we should entertain strangers. The parable of the Good Samaritan carries clear implications that we are to show neighborly concern for those who have fallen on misfortune. And many other passages instruct us to care for those in need.

The very fact that the gospel is based on forgiveness and sensitive understanding makes the church an easy victim of a manipulator. The criminal can take advantage of these traits—and some criminals seem to delight in doing so.

Of course, the skilled con man is smart enough to read the same Scriptures that Christians do! The effective manipulator learns or adapts to our trigger points. He may mimic familiar church vocabulary, or he can pitch his "needs" to appeal to sympathetic church people. His symptoms can be childlike. He can appeal to the church for basic necessities, claiming he has no place to live, nothing to eat, nothing to wear. He may request money for an invalid mother or a sick child's operation. Generous church people easily respond to such vulnerable traits.

Many church people tend to be trusting, hopeful, sympathetic, and—unfortunately—naive. They are apt to accept people at face value, believing their stories and testimonies—especially if the person in question mimics church vocabulary.[2] If an ex-offender is determined to manipulate, what better place than in the church?

The convict or ex-offender can study the patterns of the church and become very skilled at manipulation. I once received a letter quite by mistake. A prisoner had put a letter in the wrong envelope, and as a result I received a letter he had written to another prisoner who was soon to be released. Essentially, he was telling his friend how to manipulate religious volunteers. He told him what kinds of Christian words to use, encouraging him to call people "brother" and "sister" and to talk about "love" and "forgiveness." Specifically, the inmate discussed Wheaton College students. He said, "You know, these kids got rich parents. Find out where they live. Get their addresses. They got to have a lot of stuff in their house."

Of course, these unsuspecting students were conducting Bible studies, tutoring, and praying with inmates in various institutions. Their intentions were honorable and rooted in the gospel. But there was at least one prisoner whose only motive in developing a relationship was to con these students and even, eventually, to burglarize their homes.

I believe the inmate's mistake in putting the letter in the wrong envelope was providential, an act of God. I have since used this incident as an example in my training and orientation of religious volunteers—to show how a prisoner or ex-offender can use religious vocabulary to trick church people. In addition to using the "right" lingo, a skilled manipulator can adopt postures, facial expressions, and even emotions to look convincing.

Ex-offender and prison ministry leader Harry Greene warns,

> An ex-offender who wants to manipulate will find it easier in the church. He will pick his mark, usually the elderly. The young are normally skeptical but older Christians respond to a moving conversion. He will strike up a friendship with the older man or woman, who may be lonely and are easier to con. He starts by observing their jewelry, their clothes, and their cars. When invited to their home, he makes mental inventory of their possessions.
>
> Eventually, his intention is to steal. It may be a burglary; however, an ex-offender using a pseudo relationship is more likely to forge checks, commit credit card fraud, or simply persuade the elderly church member to make a large donation to a nonexistent ministry.[3]

The Temptation to Manipulate

What is the ex-offender's motive for pulling a con job on the local church? More often than not, it is the old compulsion for instant gratification.

One ex-offender who grew up in the harsh streets of the inner city with no father told me how difficult it was to find a job since he was a high-school dropout. The models for success on the streets were the pimps and drug dealers who wore flashy rings and gold chains, carried thousands of dollars in their pockets, and rode in large luxury cars. And the ex-offender told me, "It is hard to go to work for minimum wage at McDonald's when you have been making $3,500 a day as a drug dealer."

Instant gratification is part of our culture. We see it on television and on billboards. Once when I was speaking at Cabrini Green, a housing project in Chicago's inner city, I noticed a large billboard advertising the Illinois state lottery. The advertisement promised instant riches, luxurious possessions, and world travel. And it had been especially adapted to that community; it featured African-American faces.

The temptation to manipulate is basically rooted in materialism. I once knew an ex-offender who defrauded a chaplain, the greatest friend he had ever had, out of thousands of dollars. Why would he do such a thing? It may have been as simple as needing money to support a drug habit or just wanting to acquire possessions without working for them. Or he may have had more temptation in his path than he could resist.

Basic self-centeredness is another factor in tempting an ex-offender to manipulate church members who are trying to help him. If an ex-offender is focused on himself, he is not really thinking about the harm or damage he does to the people around him.

Yet another factor may be the influence of old friends or acquaintances either from prison or from the old neighborhood. An ex-offender who has become involved with a local congregation may be contacted by people he knew previously and talked into pulling a con job.

154

The Sociopathic Personality

Fortunately, the type of ex-offender that poses the greatest danger to the church is also the most rare. This is the man or woman with an antisocial personality disorder—the sociopath.[4] There are definitely people who exhibit this pathology in our communities and in our churches, and some of them come from prison. Although they make up only a small proportion of the ex-offender population, some criminals have sociopathic personalities, and such people thrive on deceiving church people.[5]

Sociopathic individuals often exhibit the following traits and characteristics:

- They lack respect for the rights of other people.
- They have an unformed conscience and are unable to feel shame and guilt.
- They are unable to form long-term and consistent relationships and commitments or to remain in consistent localities over the long term.
- They are pathological liars.
- They are skillful at charm and manipulation.
- When they are caught in deception, they can convincingly express remorse or give eloquent promises of reform—without meaning either.
- They may be very intelligent.
- They talk about emotions convincingly and can appear to be responding on an emotional level, but without actually feeling the emotions.
- They receive pleasure from manipulating other people.
- They derive excitement or stimulation from committing crimes.

An intelligent sociopath will do his homework. If he is going to encounter you, he will actually do research about what you like, what you respond to, what turns you on, and what turns you off. He will quote C. S. Lewis to a theologian. He will quote Freud to a psychologist. He will discuss fine points of the law with an attorney. He has a chameleonlike ability to adapt to his environment in order to survive.

A sociopath is always a placater; he will tell you what you want to hear. In this sense, a novice volunteer or church leader may believe a relationship is building because the sociopath makes every attempt to please him.

For this reason, I would suggest that being super-agreeable is a danger sign. Any healthy relationship involves disagreements; in fact, it is the process of working out those differences that builds relationships. But a true sociopath will keep maneuvering and adapting, trying hard never to displease you.

The sociopath is the center of his own universe. He is totally ego centered, and that is the reason he feels nothing for his victim. If he should turn to crime, his predominant concern is in not being caught and sent to prison.

What makes a sociopath especially dangerous is his ability to appear normal—mimicking appropriate behavior and displaying emotions he does not feel. Serial murderer Ted Bundy, described in an earlier chapter, was charming, polite, well dressed, and well mannered. Yet he was able to kill a succession of young women mercilessly.

John Wayne Gacy, who killed more than twenty-nine young men, was able to mingle with politicians and police and had marched in a parade with then first lady, Rosalynn Carter. He even volunteered his time as a clown at children's hospitals.

When Jeffrey Dahmer was arrested in July 1991 for murdering and mutilating more than seventeen men and boys, everyone asked, "How could he have done such horrible things and yet keep functioning?" He greeted his neighbors, he rode the bus, he worked forty hours a week—and he killed a succession of people. Obviously he possessed both work skills and social skills. Just as obviously, something was deeply wrong.

Of the more than seven hundred offenders I worked with during my years in the criminal justice system, I only met six people who fit this profile—but meeting them was a chilling experience!

The Sociopathic Teens

Late one evening two teenagers hunted down a man in his early sixties and stabbed him in excess of fifty-seven times. They stabbed him over a three-hour period. Most of the wounds were superficial, but he died of exsanguination, or total blood loss, while trying to flee his persecutors. He left a trail of blood around a golf course.

At the time of the murder, I was assistant superintendent of a maximum security juvenile detention facility. I was called early that morning and informed that the police had brought the two juveniles, ages fifteen and sixteen, to my institution. On the short drive to the facility, I wondered what kind of "monsters" these young men were.

Before arriving at the detention facility, I stopped at the crime lab just a short distance away. A lab assistant showed me the victim's shirt with its multiple stab wounds. There were so many holes and so much blood that the T-shirt and outer shirt had become meshed together and could not be pulled apart. Dried blood had saturated the garment. I visually examined the weapon, a sharp hunting knife with a five-inch blade. Seeing evidence of the crime only accelerated my imagination regarding these murderers.

Eventually, I entered my facility and went to a control room with its large glass windows overlooking a common area. Since other young criminals had been brought in the night before, I was not sure which ones to look for. A staff member gestured, "There they are." To my amazement, these two young men were calmly seated at a table playing Monopoly—less than ten hours after committing a gruesome murder.

Those young men were eventually convicted and both sent to prison for more than forty years. But they were in my custody for the two-and-a-half years of the trial procedure. During this time, I tried to gain some understanding as to the motive for the crime. But even today, I must confess that I don't have a clue what prompted their violent behavior.

Never once during those two and a half years did I see any indication of remorse for the crime or compassion for the victim. They

157

were sometimes sad because they had been deprived of their freedom and because they would be going to prison. They were never sad because of what they did.

How was this possible? Did these young men have a history of abuse? Did they come from bad homes? Were they a part of some violent neighborhood gang? The answer to all of these was no. They both came from stable families. One was the son of a teacher. Both families attended church. These teens were both good students and had no prior criminal records.

How then do we explain such a violent crime? I truly don't know, except to say that each of these young men fit the profile of a sociopath, someone without conscience.

Not All Sociopaths Go to Prison

Many would believe that a true sociopath would have to end up in prison, but that is not always the case. It is entirely possible that there are sociopathic personalities in the church today who have never served one day in prison, so I am not suggesting that all sociopathic personalities have come through corrections or the criminal justice system.

Some sociopaths do go to prison, of course, but many are able to circumvent the system because they are such superb manipulators. They quickly learn the types of words professionals want to hear and use them without genuine depth, meaning, or emotion. Therefore, a true sociopath can sound genuinely remorseful and make great promises of change and reform to the parole board without any intention of changing his ways.

We need only remember that Jeffrey Dahmer committed most of his crimes while he was on parole. He had previously gone to prison for molesting a minor and yet had written an eloquent letter to the sentencing judge telling him he had learned his lesson, would be a model citizen, and would never break the law again. It sounded convincing, but Dahmer's later actions proved his letter was nothing but lies and manipulation.

Profile of a Sociopath

I once interviewed a murderer who fit the sociopathic profile to a remarkable degree. I first saw him in the courtroom during his arraignment, but I didn't pick him out as the offender. I knew the crime. I knew the type of person I was looking for. Yet all I saw in the courtroom were attorneys dressed in expensive suits and feverishly taking notes on legal pads. The murderer I would later talk with was seated at the defendant's table, mimicking the appearance and mannerisms of the defense attorneys. This man was forty-five years of age, Caucasian, and a former mortician. He was also an ex-offender who had served six years in prison for murdering his first wife. I will call him Richard.

When I spoke with Richard, I could easily see that he was intelligent, articulate, charming, and also very calculating as to his choice of words. Often I can learn a lot about an offender by what subjects he avoids. In this case, most of the conversation centered on himself—his feelings and his reactions to the events around him. He rarely mentioned his wife. Since I was in the process of preparing a report for the court, he was clever enough to know that what he said could be used for or against him. He was not about to slip up. I consider myself perceptive, but this man was a challenge even to me, and I am convinced that he was sufficiently skilled to be able to manipulate many professionals. To illustrate this, here are the facts in his case.

Richard is currently serving a life term for murdering his second wife, whom I will call Janice. The actual events demonstrate real sociopathic behavior. While Richard was in prison serving his first murder sentence, Janice was his social worker. She was attracted to his intelligence and charmed by his romantic words and was so convinced he was a changed person that she worded her reports to appeal to the parole board for his early release. Soon they were in love—or at least she was in love with him. They were married promptly after his release.

Her naked body was found in a ditch late one night, two days after she had been reported missing. Richard never pled guilty, but the jury convicted him of murdering her.

159

Here are the facts that emerged during the trial: Richard murdered Janice by hitting her over the head repeatedly with a ball-peen hammer (a hammer with a rounded head). He meticulously shampooed the carpet, removing all traces of blood. Next, he put Janice's body in the bathtub, shampooed her hair, then drained her body of excessive fluid and blood. (Remember, Richard was a mortician by profession.) He washed her entire body, even cleaning under her nails to remove any traces of his skin or clothing fragments. Next, he stuffed her body into the trunk of their car and drove to a remote place, where he unceremoniously dumped her into a ditch.

Richard then invited his mother-in-law and brother-in-law to his apartment. He told them there had been an argument and that his wife had stormed out. But Janice's mother noticed her daughter's eyeglasses in the living room. Janice could not see without those glasses, and her mother knew that she would never walk off without them.

Throughout the funeral, the victim's family noticed that Richard exhibited no emotion unless someone was actually looking at him. He put his head in his hands and pretended he was crying, but members of the family were not convinced it was genuine.

Forensic science proved to be Richard's undoing. Using microscopes, lab technicians found the victim's smashed hairs embedded on the head of the hammer. Next the investigators lifted the carpet. Although he had cleaned well, blood of Janice's type had saturated the wood and padding beneath the carpeting. Finally, a bit of rubber molding found in Janice's hair was connected to the trunk of Richard's auto.

Several professionals were manipulated by Richard's charm, including Janice, the parole board that voted for his release, and the judge that finally approved the early release. If professionals can be lured by a sociopath into decisions that resulted in a new crime, the average church volunteer must be extremely vigilant, asking the Holy Spirit for discernment, and utilizing the collective wisdom of the church leaders. I have no evidence that church volunteers worked with Richard while he was incarcerated or that he ever made any claims to being religious. But I do believe he could have manipulated and deceived many church volunteers just as easily as he deceived Janice.

Since initially volunteers are convinced of a person's sincerity by their words, Richard would have quickly adapted to his hearers and probably said all the right words. He would have expressed sorrow for his past crimes. He would have made eloquent promises about his intention to reform and about future goals. I'm convinced he would also have used the right church language, seasoned with emotion, to convince his hearer he was truly "born again."

Because sociopaths like Richard actually seem to enjoy manipulating other people, it is hard to know how many who go to prison actually improve on release.[6] A study by Rarendosson and Hein in 1959 indicated that the improvement rate of a sociopath after imprisonment is about 50 percent, but the author also noted that it was difficult to know if the individuals had truly changed or had simply become more skilled at avoiding arrest.

Is a Sociopath Beyond Help?

I do not want to deny the possibility that with true confession and repentance the grace of God can work in Richard, Jeffrey Dahmer, or any other sociopath to turn him away from his sin. The Bible makes it clear that it's never too late for anyone to turn to God.

Recently I was lecturing at Dallas Baptist University, and most of the students were police officers enrolled in a criminal justice night class that applied to their continuing education. I detected that some were not believers. Their basic attitude about criminals was predictably suspicious and cynical. When I asked them, "Do you believe there is any category of offender beyond hope?" many of them raised their hands and volunteered their thoughts. Some said, "Child molesters." Others said, "Serial murderers." Together they made a long list of offenders who in their estimation were "too far gone" to turn around. Even several Christian officers said, "God won't save some criminals."[7]

161

My response to that last remark was to talk about an innocent Jesus dying on a cross next to two criminals who deserved to be there. Even the criminals had been mocking Jesus. But suddenly one of the criminals comes to his senses:

> One of the criminals hanging beside him scoffed, "So you're the Messiah, are you? Prove it by saving yourself—and us, too, while you're at it!" . . . But the other criminal protested. "Don't you even fear God when you are dying? We deserve to die for our evil deeds, but this man hasn't done one thing wrong." Then he said, "Jesus, remember me when you come into your Kingdom." And Jesus replied, "Today you will be with me in Paradise. This is a solemn promise." (Luke 23:39–43 LB)

Certainly that condemned criminal was not saved by his life or his deeds. It was his expression of faith that saved him.

I have used this passage hundreds of times when speaking before prisoners. What a joy it is to see the expression on a prisoner's face who has never read the Bible or is not familiar with this interaction between a dying Savior and a saved criminal! In this particular instance, however, the passage had a different effect. After I gave this illustration in the class, the police officers who had made up the list were conspicuously silent.

If we take God's Word seriously, we must "never say never" about anybody, even a sociopath. However, that doesn't mean that churches can't take precautions to protect themselves from the deadly manipulations of a sociopath. God tells us that his Spirit will give us wisdom if we ask for it. But we need to ask!

The Huckster—A Religious Con Man

One of my deepest concerns about ex-offenders who manipulate the church has to do with those who are elevated to leadership positions in the church. It is not uncommon for churches to ordain an ex-offender or promote him to church leadership within the first year without really knowing the authenticity of his background. Manipulators and deceivers have been elevated to such positions in contradiction to the admonitions of Scripture.

One reason for special vigilance in preventing this is that the leaders are the most visible aspect of the church to the unbelieving world. My friend Dick Rohrer, vice president of Bill Glass Ministries, once told me about a time he was an airline passenger. He introduced himself to a fellow passenger, who asked, "What kind of work do you do?"

Dick replied, "I am an evangelist."

The man responded, "Oh, you are one of *those* people!" The derogatory tone clearly reflected the man's bias.

Many nonbelievers in our society are cynical about religious leaders. Many public opinion polls have indicated that people rate the credibility of a televangelist below that of a used-car salesman! And unfortunately, some of these suspicions are grounded in reality.

Sinclair Lewis's famous novel, *Elmer Gantry*,[8] which was later made into a popular film starring Burt Lancaster, paints a classic picture of a religious huckster. Gantry, the central figure of the piece, used charm and religious lingo to obtain money while simultaneously leading a sinful life. Since then, a series of other books and pictures, such as *Paper Moon* and more recently *Leap of Faith*, have depicted hucksters who use religious promises to defraud people of their money.

But the concept of a religious huckster[9] predates Sinclair Lewis. It is found in the Bible. The apostle Paul, in 2 Corinthians 2:17, makes reference to certain people (presumably evangelists) who were more interested in making money than furthering the kingdom of God. The Living Bible uses the word *huckster*. In addition, 1 Timothy 6:5–8 warns of preachers who preach for profit and self-gain but not for the kingdom of God. The writer says emphatically "Keep away from them" (LB).

The Edmund Lopes Story

A shocking story dramatically illustrates what can happen when a church fails to use reasonable prudence in the face of a religious con. In 1960, a man named Edmund Lopes molested a boy in Brockton, Massachusetts. (At the time he was using the alias Jasper Brown.) He served a prison term for the crime, then moved to the Midwest after his release.

163

In 1972, Lopes was convicted by a jury of murdering his wife in Bloomingdale, Illinois. He had committed this crime in 1970, within a year of their wedding date, burying her body in a vacant lot. On the same day he attempted to kill his girlfriend by strangling her with a rope, stabbing her, and throwing her down a flight of stairs. He then fled to Florida, but was brought back to Illinois to stand trial after construction workers unearthed his wife's body. Lopes was assessed a fifty- to ninety-nine year prison sentence. The judge who sentenced him commented at the time of the hearing, "This is just about the most dastardly way that a crime of this nature can be committed!"

Lopes was paroled in 1983 but immediately violated his parole by moving to the state of Washington several days after his release. This was no vacation or pleasure trip; Lopes was deliberately fleeing the jurisdiction of his parole. (This was the crime that would eventually send him back to prison.)

From this point on, Lopes began a systematic pattern of pathological lies and seeking religious marks. He took a job as a medical-supply salesman and joined the First Baptist Church in the little town of West Richland, Washington. After a three-year period, however, the church became so enamored with him as a lay leader, they asked him to become the church's pastor. He accepted the position and was ordained by the church, although they knew little about his background.

Lopes never told the church about his particular criminal past or his fugitive status. Instead, Lopes concocted an elaborate—and false—testimony. He told the church congregation he had been a hit man for the Mafia and had killed twenty-eight people. He also explained that he had become a Christian through the counseling of Billy Graham. The congregation accepted Lopes's mob story and rejoiced that God had forgiven him in a powerful way. Said one of the church members, Tammy LaPlant, "Personally, I never questioned what he told us. I just assumed it was true."

Lopes's pride was eventually his undoing. He began to share his story as a mob enforcer more frequently. A local newspaper reporter, who happened to visit the church began to check old newspapers and unearthed Lopes's real past. She also discovered that a warrant had been issued for his arrest and informed the police. Harold Rivkin, Bloomingdale's former chief of police, remembered Lopes as a drifter who had used many aliases to escape the law. "His was quite a con job, I've got to tell you," said Rivkin.

Some of the churchgoers in Lopes's tiny congregation were devastated. They realized that the pastor's secret identity meant that his work with them was built on lies. Yet many defended Lopes, insisting that he had done much good in the community. He had been an influential community leader, even serving as an umpire for Little League games.

In 1992, Lopes found himself back in an Illinois jail. "This man is a new man," he told the parole board, insisting that he had learned from his mistakes. According to Lopes, "I told people I was a Mafia hit man so they would respect me. To say that a man was transformed after being in this Mafia organization; that is a great thing!"

Lopes wanted the parole board to let him walk free, even as it became apparent that Lopes had not only lied to his congregation about his past, but had also lied to his new wife and his trusted friends. In the meantime, word came that police in Brockton, Massachusetts, wanted to question Lopes about the death of another former girlfriend. (Lopes had told two ministers and a reporter he had killed a woman in Massachusetts, but then had refused to talk to police about this statement.)

Even after Lopes had been extradited to Illinois, some members of his church board and other coworkers continued to defend their pastor. Some still insist that he is a wonderful man. In fact, although the First Baptist Church no longer considers Lopes to be their pastor, some of his loyal parishioners have formed a new church, The Cross of Christ Bible Church, which meets in homes. They have called Edmund Lopes to be their pastor, but they may have to wait many years before his release.

One defense the people of Lopes's church make is that "he did a lot of good." I do not doubt this claim. It is quite possible to "do good" on one level while at the same time committing horrible crimes. But the bottom line is that Edmund Lopes lived a lie and that a ministry based on lies is totally inconsistent with a Christian and minister of the gospel. He was standing before the church

165

as an example of a disciple of Jesus Christ and preaching from the Bible to his parishioners, yet his testimony was false. He was a fugitive from justice. He had hidden a past murder and other past crimes. These two facts oppose one another. They cannot be reconciled!

In my opinion, Lopes subsequently has but one correct series of choices to make:

- He must immediately resign as a pastor.
- He must plead guilty to evading parole.
- He must accept a judge's sentence to return to prison.
- He must repent and be honest before God.
- He must sincerely apologize to his friends, his wife, and his congregation whom he lied to and manipulated. He must seek their forgiveness.

Lopes is, in my estimation, still locked into a pattern of skillful manipulation and has not pursued this correct series of choices. Once arrested, he immediately informed the parole board he was "a new man." But he obviously did this to escape any consequences for behavior. He kept trying to escape discipline and avoided taking responsibility for his actions. He fabricated an elaborate rationalization for the Mafia story, pleading "it really didn't hurt anyone." But it was more heartwarming and convincing a testimony than telling people you had murdered your wife, buried her body, and attempted to murder your girlfriend, then violated parole and disappeared.

I consider this individual a dangerous man, a sociopath. Why? I see little evidence of true repentance or change in his life. I do not see any outward indication that this man has made a true commitment to follow Christ. Without it, he is likely to continue his pattern of lying, manipulation, and perhaps even violence. What concerns me most is that rather than renouncing his role as a minister of the gospel and as a pastor, he goes on to form a new church. I would like to suggest this type of deception is an isolated case, but I know it is not as evidenced by the Rev. Walker Railey case of Dallas. Cons and manipulations, unfortunately, do not stop at the pulpit!

Don't Give Up on Ministry

All these stories of crime and manipulation might well make church members and leadership a little wary of prison and after-care ministry. So I want to stress that such massive manipulation is *not* the rule in working with prisoners and ex-offenders—especially if the church takes reasonable precautions and exercises a little discretion.

There will always be a risk in loving—a risk for the sake of the gospel. And it is a risk we must take more than once, even if we get "stung."

A pastor once told me, "We tried prison ministry several years ago, but it didn't work." Not knowing what he meant, I inquired further.

"We once had an ex-offender in our church," he replied, "but he stole someone's wallet. We never saw him again, and since then we haven't had any ex-offenders in our church."

I believe that pastor was wrong. For me, a church that says "We tried it once and it didn't work" is making an excuse that can be used with any category of hurting people—the homeless, widows, those who are hungry.

The mandate of the gospel, found in the account of the last judgment in Matthew 25 and in Hebrews 13 is not an invitation. An invitation leaves us with the option of accepting or declining. But God's call for the church to be agents of social change in ministry to hurting people is an imperative, a command. One bad experience—or even several bad experiences—does not exempt us from reaching out to ex-offenders or other hurting people.

We are to receive ex-offenders into our community and our churches. We are to forgive them as God has forgiven us. However, understanding the reality of people who can be very clever in their manipulations, it is entirely reasonable for church leaders to place a high priority on protecting both church resources and the people of their congregations.

I am not advising that we should give needy people the "third degree," but I believe we can and should exercise reasonable caution. Yes, we will make mistakes from time to time. The only way to avoid that is to stop responding to any need. If we do err in the name of mercy and compassion while exercising reasonable caution, I would say we are following the gospel mandate.

Discernment is a gift of the Holy Spirit and a resource to the church. God has promised that his Spirit will give us wisdom and discernment if we ask. But we have to ask! We must pray for this gift and then exercise it the best we can. In the next chapter we will examine some ways that the church can protect itself from manipulation while at the same time working to remain true to the call of Christ in ministering to ex-offenders.

8

Wise As Serpents
Strategies for Reducing the Risk

We saw in chapter 7 that following the gospel mandate to work with prisoners and ex-offenders automatically entails some risk of being manipulated or conned. But that doesn't mean that churches should deliberately remain naive—open to being used or manipulated. Nowhere does the gospel say we are to suspend vigilance or hang up our brains outside the church (or prison) door! Matthew 10:16, in fact, states that we are to be as "wise as serpents" as well as "harmless as doves" (NKJV).

The point of this chapter, therefore, is not to eradicate all risk in ministering to ex-offenders, but to explore some strategies by which churches can minimize the occasions for deception.

This is important not only to protect members of the sponsoring churches, but also to help the ex-offenders themselves. We do former prisoners no favor when we let them manipulate us—perhaps setting themselves up to fall back into crime—rather than holding them accountable for honesty and growth.

Strategy #1: Run a Background Check

How can the church protect itself against the manipulations of a sociopath? I believe the church can begin by being vigilant about an ex-offender's past record. So often congregations and church leaders are entirely dependent on the word of the ex-offender as he shares his background with the pastor and elders of the church. Rarely do churches make the effort to run a background check on a member.

Is it wrong to investigate an ex-offender's background? I do not believe it is, especially when the prior crimes fall into certain dangerous categories. When the crime is murder, for instance, it is good to know some details regarding the event. I am not suggesting this information should be public knowledge for the whole congregation, but certainly the pastor and the church elders, who are charged with shepherding the ex-offender's spiritual growth, should know.

These are some of the criminal histories I believe demand heightened vigilance:

- a pedophile (child molester)
- an arsonist
- someone with a habitual pattern of violence (including multiple rape, armed robbery, and battery)
- someone with a history of severe psychiatric disorder (such as psychosis, multiple personalities, or paranoid schizophrenia)

These areas are red flags, because they tend to represent patterns of behavior rather than one-time events. But they don't necessarily mean the church should shun the ex-offender. And I certainly do not mean to suggest that ex-offenders in these categories cannot change by the power of God. I have seen dramatic evidence of such change in the lives of regenerate ex-offenders.

The presence of these kinds of crime in an ex-offender's background simply indicates the need for closer attention to his activities and ongoing growth. It would be a great burden for a pastor and his church board if an arsonist was accepted into fellowship with no questions asked and then burned down the church or the homes of members of the congregation! Acts of violence or disruptive behavior from an unstable and disturbed ex-offender could upset worship services and eventually the unity of the church body.

What if the crime was murder? Strangely enough, I would be less concerned about most murders than I would be about certain other crimes. Statistically speaking, crimes such as burglary are far more likely to be repeated by released prisoners than are homicides.

Most homicides occur under one of three conditions. *Involuntary manslaughter* is usually the result of recklessness or irresponsibility; killing someone while driving drunk falls into this category. It is certainly a serious offense, but if the church has evidence that the person has sought treatment for the underlying problem—for instance, a drinker has become involved in Alcoholics Anonymous—the chance of that crime being repeated is really minimal.

A second form of homicide is the so-called *crime of passion*. Many of these murders occur in domestic situations—individuals kill their wives, husbands, neighbors, and friends when gripped by an intense emotion such as anger or jealousy. People engaged in domestic violence are often under the influence of alcohol or drugs at the time of the crime. If the ex-offender has moved significantly toward emotional maturity, this crime is unlikely to repeat itself. The key factor with this sort of crime would be close mentoring and shepherding within the church structure regarding expressions of anger and hostility.

A third form of homicide is the *premeditated murder.* The criminal planned it, and he tried to execute the crime in such a way as not to get caught. This crime may involve a killing for hire. Even in such cases, the ex-offender may have a good chance of avoiding a repeat offense.

In 1990 I met a prisoner named Danny Duchene who fit this category. A man in his early twenties, he had been recruited by organized crime when he was nineteen years old and had been paid a mere five hundred dollars to kill a man he did not know. At the time, Danny had been addicted to drugs and would have

171

done anything to get money for the substances he craved. Certainly the organized crime people who approached him and solicited the murder had known and taken advantage of Danny's psychological and physical state. But when I met Danny, he was finally drug free and a growing Christian. I do not believe that someone like Danny would present a threat to society as a future murderer.

There is one final category of homicide that does concern me— the murders committed by the type of *sociopathic* criminals profiled in the previous chapter. This individual can kill without any guilt feelings. In fact, sociopathic murderers I have known and interviewed tend to see their victims as objects, not people. This type of person, who for some reason has no sense of the rights and value of another human being, is likely to be a repeat offender. A thorough background check is likely to reveal the pattern of a sociopath and alert the church leaders to be especially vigilant in shepherding this ex-offender.

Because the same crime can indicate a number of varying circumstances, it is important to investigate the facts. How long ago did the crime take place? How long has the ex-offender been a Christian? If he was recently released, what does the prison chaplain say regarding his growth? An ex-offender who committed a single murder in the heat of passion or under the influence of alcohol may pose less of a risk than a habitual thief whose arrests reveal a pattern of escalating violence.

Strategy #2: Observe Behaviors, Not Just Words

Isaiah 55:7 says, "Let men cast off their wicked deeds; let them banish from their minds the very thought of doing wrong! Let them turn to the Lord that he may have mercy upon them, and to our God, for he will abundantly pardon!" (LB). And Ephesians 4:28 echoes, "He who has been stealing must steal no longer." These verses, of course, set down a correct standard for all ex-offenders who become a part of the local church. Christians must expect and demand a change in *behaviors*—not just a verbal testimony.

Of course, an ex-offender's words are the first sign a prison ministry volunteer or a church leader is likely to have that an ex-offender has changed and intends to follow Christ. But this can be a problem, because a skilled manipulator can fake the words that bring him acceptance in a church. For instance, I have no doubt that Richard, the sociopathic murderer whose story I told in the previous chapter, would have quickly adapted to his hearers and probably said all the right words. He would have expressed sorrow for his past crimes. He would have made eloquent promises about his intention to reform and about future goals. I'm convinced he would also have used the right church language, seasoned with emotion, to convince his hearer he was truly "born again."

Are we to disbelieve every criminal who expresses remorse? How are we to know who is genuine? How can we know the faker from the real thing? In fact, we only know who is authentic through the test of time, and that translates into watching behaviors. Even a sociopath will not be able to hold his act together forever.

But isn't there a risk to the church in waiting for someone potentially dangerous to slip up? Yes, there is, unless we take reasonable precautions. If churches properly supervise an ex-offender, support him through a mentoring relationship, and shepherd his growth as a Christian, not much time will go by before there is evidence in one direction or another—evidence either of growth or of backsliding. The key factor is support and close supervision.

What kind of behaviors give evidence of growth?

Many prisoners, for instance, are chronic smokers. I would not hinge the authenticity of a prisoner's belief on this alone; however, I would certainly observe whether the regenerate ex-offender is making a sincere attempt to stop such a destructive habit.

Another area of improvement to observe is a reduction in the use of profanity. I always advise volunteers not to become shocked by occasional slips of the tongue; old habits will not be broken overnight. As time goes on, however, some definite change should be observable in this area.

Volunteers should also be aware of how the prisoner talks about his problems. Blaming other people for his problems, venting anger or even outrage at officials, or wallowing in self-pity can all be indications that growth has slowed.

Another significant change in behavior and attitude involves how the inmate accepts and is willing to be guided by authority, as expressed in Romans 13:1–3. (This means *all* authority, not just that of chaplains and church leaders.) I know Christian inmates who routinely pray for the warden, the officers, and other officials who administer the prison. This is a very good sign! In a sense, it is literally making peace with enemies.

One of the most important behavioral indicators of change is that of reaching out to others. A person who is growing in Christ will begin living in the spirit of the first chapter of 2 Corinthians, in which Paul discusses how Christians should show comfort to others as comfort has been shown to them. Most Christian ex-offenders have been shown ample love and caring from both chaplains and volunteers. If they are sincere in their reform and repentance, they will begin reaching out to other hurting people, such as the homeless in their communities and other ex-offenders.

Yet another crucial measure of behavioral change has to do with accountability. And again, this doesn't just mean words of remorse (which can easily be faked). Churches need to look for signs that the ex-offender is facing the reality of what he did. Is he focusing attention on the victim and the victim's family, or is he primarily interested in himself? In my estimation, an offender who cries and moans about his incarceration, his loss of freedom, and his loss of family but fails to pay attention to the losses of the victim or the victim's family is not demonstrating proper accountability.

An important part of accountability is the willingness to make restitution[1] for damage that has been done. This is a biblically based concept that can bring healing. I believe it is also a sign of significant emotional and spiritual growth—provided the restitution efforts come at the offender's own initiative and that he remains committed to making restitution.

There are many ways of damaging a victim that go beyond injury or death. A burglar violates the victim's sense of security and personal space. Thieves deprive victims of their possessions, even treasured possessions such as irreplaceable photographs and heirlooms. Rapists inflict acute psychological damage that can last for years, if not a lifetime. And injury reaches beyond the immediate victim as well. For instance, small children who witness the assault or death of a parent can sustain long-lasting psychological and emotional harm.

The possible forms of restitution can be just as various as the forms of damage. One form of restitution is monetary. In the case of embezzlement or a theft, the ex-offender should work to repay the money, even in small amounts of twenty-five, fifty, or a hundred dollars a month, over a period of many years.[2] Sometimes the losses are so large that the ex-offender is unable to repay the full amount or to make up for indirect losses such as potential interest earned. But the attempt is nevertheless vital because it shows that the offender cares about the victim and is willing to do what is necessary to make things right. Restitution as a gesture often has a great impact on the victim, as well as on the offender. I have seen restitution efforts result in face-to-face meetings, forgiveness, and the mending of broken relationships.

A judge in Memphis uses a creative form of restitution. Recently, after finding a man guilty of burglarizing an elderly woman's apartment and stealing her television, he allowed the woman to take anything from the offender's home of equal value, with the attorneys and the judge supervising. She took his jam box. "It wasn't worth as much as my TV," she said, "but I thought he would miss it more."

Not all victim losses are monetary, of course, and full restitution is not always possible or advisable. In the case of a violent crime like rape, I am not convinced it is wise for the victim and the offender to get together; such a meeting could cause further psychological damage to the victim. But there are other ways for the ex-offender to make amends. For instance, he could pay the cost of psychological counseling for the victim.

For some crimes, a specific victim is hard to pinpoint, but restitution may still be possible. A delinquent who has pulled up flowers in a public park or sprayed graffiti on the sides of a building can do community service—most appropriately, doing cleanup in public places. I have known juveniles who spent an entire summer planting flowers, without pay, in parks they had formerly trampled. In the process, they learned that plants take time to grow.

The restitution issue may become even more tricky in cases of crime that resulted in death. How does an ex-offender who was convicted of vehicular homicide while driving under the influence of alcohol make amends? First, the ex-offender can donate whatever resources are available to help pay the victim's funeral costs. Next, if the victim had children, the ex-offender can contribute to a fund to pay for their college education. Now, few ex-offenders could afford the forty or fifty thousand dollars it would take to complete the funds, but what is important at this point is the gesture and the sacrifice. Making whatever restitution is possible demonstrates a movement toward emotional and spiritual maturity.

Strategy #3: Watch Out for Excuses and Relabeling

Another warning sign to look for in the regenerated ex-offender is ongoing *denial or unwillingness to take responsibility* for the crime. The ex-offender who continues to make excuses for what he did or to relabel his crime is one who should be watched.

I once interviewed a man who had been convicted of multiple rape and who told me, "They were prostitutes. It didn't seem a crime." The man later came to face his sin squarely and has done well in aftercare. At the time of our interview, however, he was playing denial games, relabeling his victims to escape responsibility. In his mind, since a prostitute was committing both a crime and a sin, raping them was not a crime. And until he was able to face the reality of his crime, I believe he was in danger of falling back into criminal patterns.

"The Devil Made Me Do It"

When I speak publicly, I am frequently asked, "Don't you think some criminals are possessed by the devil?"

I do not deny the presence of evil. I acknowledge the existence of personified evil: Satan.

I also believe that many of the crimes we hear and read about have an element of satanic influence involved. I know that many criminals and prisoners actively worship Satan, and I have personally witnessed behaviors and events in several prisons that convinced me evil forces were at work.

Further, I believe that the church must always be aware of Satan's mechanizations and prepared to do battle, with God's help. Ephesians 6:12–13 clearly states: "For our struggle is not against flesh and blood, but against . . . the powers of this dark world and against the spiritual forces of evil. . . . Therefore put on the full armor of God, so that when the day of evil comes, you may be able to stand your ground."

But I also believe what C. S. Lewis said about two dangers regarding Satan. One danger is to believe Satan does not exist, but the other danger is to become too interested in him. It is possible to become preoccupied with Satan. It is also possible for ex-offenders and the churches who support them to use "evil influence" to reduce criminal responsibility.

The television comedian Flip Wilson used to say as part of a routine, "The devil made me do it." Unfortunately, that claim can easily become an excuse for criminals searching for a way to relabel their crime and escape accountability.

The stereotype of evil possession represented in the movie *The Exorcist* was not correct. According to the screenplay, an innocent young girl is minding her own business, when suddenly she is possessed by an evil spirit and driven to outrageous and violent behavior. But this is not the way it works.

Many in society assume that Jeffrey Dahmer was under possession by demonic forces when he committed his horrendous crimes of murder and mutilation. On closer examination, however, the picture emerges of a man who used his liberty to choose a particular path.

Dahmer may have worshiped Satan. He may have, as reported, created a shrine of human skulls. He may have identified with the film, *Exorcist III*, which he repeatedly watched. But I do not believe that Jeffrey Dahmer was an innocent man, leading a good moral life, who suddenly became possessed by evil! This would

177

imply he could not help himself, that he was not responsible for anything he did because "the devil made him do it."

Instead, Dahmer chose to turn away from God. He chose to satisfy his selfish drives and cravings. Dahmer was a man who made a progression of sinful choices and eventually lost self-control; eventually his sinful activities became compulsive and increasingly vile. The devil was certainly involved in his activities, but only with his complicity.

Spiritual warfare is a reality. The devil is literally seeking opportunities to snare us. Paul compares him to a "roaring lion" who "devours" his enemies. We must be vigilant enough and not give him opportunities to devastate both our church and our ministries. And yet we must not let him be used as an excuse!

"I Was Mentally Ill"

For similar reasons, I am generally opposed to the use of the insanity plea, which I believe has been abused in our courts. That plea often sends a message to offenders that the more shocking the crime, the more they can claim they were "not themselves that day," or "temporarily insane," or "driven by outside forces."

Over the years I have been concerned by the cues psychiatry sends to offenders. Both psychology and psychiatry when exercised by secular professionals can unknowingly give excuses to criminals for their behavior.

Many of the juvenile delinquents I worked with, whose crimes ranged from murder and rape to armed robbery and auto theft, had a reason or a motive for committing their crime. They may have been expressing anger toward a parent who neglected them. They may have wanted money to pay for a drug habit. They may have felt an impulse of revenge toward someone who thwarted a goal. But because I was in a position to talk with these delinquents day in and day out, in a locked setting, I knew that most of them had difficulty articulating why they committed their crimes. So I was always fascinated to observe how their communication patterns would change after a session or two with their psychiatrist.

Some of the youths would even begin using psychiatric terminology. One young man told me, "I killed my teacher because my father abused me when I was small." Another said, "I robbed the gas station because I had low self-esteem and no authority figure growing up." Still another delinquent stated, "Because I was neglected in my formative years, I took out my aggression on someone else."

This is not how teenagers talk! Terms like "aggression" and "neglect in the formative years" had to have come from professionals!

I have also heard adult criminals explaining their behaviors with terms like "obsessive-compulsive," "given to a lack of impulse control," "cognitive dissidence," "neurosis," "detached personality," "adolescent adjustment reaction," and "acute anxiety." And what was happening in these cases was quite clear. Criminals who wanted excuses and rationalizations for their behavior were actually mimicking what the professionals were saying in their analysis.

Social workers tend to look at the effects of environment and family on behaviors. Criminologists tend to look at family patterns such as the incarceration of a parent or a sibling in prison or a genetic predisposition to violence. Theologians tend to evaluate crime from the perspective of responsibility and sin. And some psychiatrists, especially non-Christian ones, "explain" criminal behavior by using a label that implies a personality disorder, a neurosis, or a mental disease. Many offenders are quick to jump at the possibility of relabeling their sin. Instead of taking responsibility for their crime, they can blame it on some hidden, primal, repressed emotion that came from early neglect.

In 1979 I was working as a probation officer with an offender who had repeatedly committed incest with his ten-year-old stepdaughter. He was initially remorseful and told me that he knew what he did was wrong. After several sessions with a psychiatrist, however, he began to link his crime with his experience as a soldier in Vietnam. He told me that every time he had sex with his young stepdaughter, he was also having an acute flashback or a reaction to the trauma he experienced on the battlefield.

What happened? I do not believe he could consciously admit his crime and continue to live with himself. So he took advantage of concepts learned in therapy and relabeled his sin.

179

I do not think these chameleonlike adaptations should surprise us. All people engage defense mechanisms to protect them from behaviors and experiences that are hurtful. These defenses may be necessary for us to be able to function from day to day. But when defense mechanisms become tools for escaping responsibility, they not only get in the way of growth; they can also set an ex-offender up for a recurrence of the negative behavior.

Strategy #4: Confront in Love

I believe that church leaders and mentors are called to a ministry of "reality therapy" for ex-offenders—to strip away all excuses, all phony labels, and all professional rationalizations that reduce personal accountability and responsibility for criminal and manipulative behaviors.

When approached in the right spirit, confrontation is loving behavior! It is honest communication to look at an ex-offender directly and say, "I have serious doubts about what you are telling me" or "I will not do that." That is far better than smiling and allowing oneself to be pandered or placated. An ex-offender, like anyone, will make mistakes. If we love him, we will want to correct him, not ignore inappropriate or dishonest behaviors.

After visiting a prisoner at the local jail, I received a call the next day from his defense attorney. The attorney informed me that I was being subpoenaed to be a character witness on the prisoner's behalf at a sentencing. I do not believe volunteers in prison ministry should be involved in writing letters to parole boards, or being a character witness on behalf of an offender unless under extraordinary circumstances (such as having known the person over a long period of time).

I informed the attorney that I would respond to the subpoena but would state in open court that I was being manipulated by his client and that I had only known him for a total of forty-five minutes. Not surprisingly, the attorney informed me that my services would not be required.

Manipulation usually starts on a small level and escalates. When we catch the little things, confrontation in love is essential. An

180

ex-offender who manipulates will start by getting other people to do his work for him. It may be as simple as "Could you get those forms for me?" or "Could you fill this out?" or "You are much better at writing."

I once had an offender call me from jail with a very simple request: "Could you visit me?" I was happy to comply. But within two days his requests had escalated to "Could you go to my car, which is impounded (thirty miles from where I lived), get some of my clothes and papers out of the trunk, and bring them back to me? And could you lend me some money so I can get my car back?"

I had no problem putting the brakes on these additional requests. I was not going to begin running errands for a stranger. We had built no trust, nor had he established credibility. I was certainly not going to lend him any money!

One of the surest ways to protect the local church from manipulation is to say no when such an answer is appropriate. Not only does an honest answer help keep the ex-offender honest, but churches also have limited resources, and we do not always use those resources most wisely when we respond to every "need" that comes to the front door of the church. We need leaders who will be good stewards of the church's resources and determine where those resources should best be used.

Strategy #5: Don't Put Ex-Offenders in Areas of Known Weakness

I cannot stress too strongly the importance of not giving ex-offenders responsibilities in the areas of their known weaknesses.

I recall so many instances in which a church celebrated the reformation of an ex-offender but then set him up for failure by putting him right in the line of his greatest temptation.

As a probation officer, I once worked with a pedophile (a child molester) who was one of the most clever manipulators I have ever met. He earned a master's degree in human services, became well established in the community by working for the local government, and became licensed as a daycare operator—all so he could have opportunity to fulfill his sinful desires. After his conviction he joined a church and made a public confession of his sin. This church rejoiced that God had healed a child molester.

Now, I will not attempt to judge whether or not that man's confession was sincere. I do believe the church erred, however, in eventually making him the director of the church's daycare center. Before the church put a stop to his activities, the judge did. The judge said to the ex-offender in open court, "I would no sooner have you at playgrounds or working in a daycare center than I would give an alcoholic a job as a wine taster!" He was forbidden to work in the daycare center or go near playgrounds.

I believe the judge's ruling was appropriate and showed wisdom. If any Christian has an identified pattern of sin, we are not to put him in harm's way; we are not to seek out the temptation. It is a form of pride to strut in the face of potential sin just to demonstrate the degree of our reformation. When there is an area of known weakness, the church has an obligation to shelter and protect ex-offenders and to counsel them in ways that would redirect their activities, not put them in the line of direct temptation.

In the same way, I believe it is possible for God to heal someone of alcoholism, either directly or through a program such as Alcoholics Anonymous. But I certainly doubt that the recovered alcoholic would be prudent to take a job as a bartender!

Several years ago, an ex-offender who worked for a prison ministry—a very talented and valuable worker—became involved in a protracted pattern of sexual sin. The ministry would send him alone on trips to faraway cities. Because the ministry knew he had a history of promiscuity before his conversion, I believe they should have been wise enough to send him with a traveling companion. I believe he got involved in patterns of adultery and immorality because he was put in a position of his known weakness.

Strategy #6: Use Discernment in Putting Ex-Offenders in Positions of Leadership

How can churches protect themselves from ex-offenders who take positions of leadership and perpetuate religious cons? Several commonsense measures can be taken.

The first point should be fairly evident. It's especially important to do a background check on any ex-offender who is being considered for a leadership position. The church in Washington that ordained Edmund Lopes made no effort to track his educational or personal history. They didn't even check out his testimony about being imprisoned for serving as a Mafia hit man. (Records about court convictions and prison terms are public and accessible.) Instead, they simply accepted his word. And while this approach may work nine times out of ten, it can also open the door for a true manipulator to con an entire congregation.

Newspaper articles will not necessarily be trustworthy as evidence of someone's true past. I remember a time when a major prison ministry was planning to feature a certain ex-offender in their newsletter. This man claimed to have fought in Vietnam and to have been greatly decorated, and he supported his claims with newspaper clippings from his hometown. But an officer who had served in Vietnam happened to read a proof of the newsletter article and challenged its authenticity. He said that no troops had been fighting in Vietnam in the specific place and time that the ex-offender claimed to have fought. And sure enough, it turned out the ex-offender had never even been to Vietnam. He had simply lied to the reporters of his hometown paper, and they had repeated the lies.

Another commonsense measure would be to check the individual's track record of leadership in the church. Most churches accept as their pastor someone who has shown leadership either as a deacon or an elder, served as the pastor of another church, or served in churches while attending school.

Yet another commonsense measure would be to avoid appointing an ex-offender to a position of leadership in the church for a period of time—at least three years. Such a waiting period would give the ex-offender time to grow and to exhibit spiritual and emotional growth through his behavior.

In addition, I believe that ex-offenders should not be ordained without an extensive course of study. I have met many ex-offenders who call themselves "ordained," "reverend," "ministers," or "pastors." I have met ex-offenders who have not gone to college or to seminary but who insist that "God ordained me

183

for ministry." Yet while I believe that God does give individuals gifts to share within the church, I also believe the church has good reason to pose high standards for ordination. This could mean either degrees from a respectable college and seminary or a rigorous program of examination within the church itself.

When a man or woman displays a diploma from an accredited four-year college, we can assume that certain things have happened. We know that the individual has been required to read books, write papers, enter into classroom discussion, and exhibit proficiency in his or her chosen subjects. We can assume that he or she has gained a required number of credit hours, studied a balanced curriculum. And we can have assurance that the faculty and the courses meet certain standards.

By the same token, if we see that someone has graduated from an accredited law school or received a degree in medicine from a respected medical school, we can assume that his or her training has been comprehensive. We can assume that mentors have guided his knowledge and his skill.

We can summarize all this by saying that a college degree, a seminary degree, or both give a certain indication that an individual is trustworthy and competent. This does not mean that he or she cannot sin or act unethically! But the certification process itself tells us the individual is ready and able to perform in his or her chosen profession.

I personally feel that "ordination by mail" or the ordination by a local assembly without rigorous teaching and examination is dangerous. The ex-offender will be tempted to use his title in a way that will imply he has taken the same educational route as the pastor of a church in a mainline denomination.

In other words, the quick ordination can be another form of manipulation—obtaining a credential without actually paying dues. Accepting such an ordination can reinforce the tendency on the part of some ex-offenders to seek shortcuts, to get the titles and reputation without taking the established route. It can become a quick way for the ex-offender to become a minister or a pastor without having his thinking tested by biblical scholars and excellent teachers in an established orthodox seminary.

184

I know there are many people who are effective in ministry and in evangelism but have not gone to college or seminary. And yet I believe the process of going to a good seminary after being grounded in biblical studies and philosophy at an excellent college is the best route whenever possible. Such studies discipline the mind, for one thing. And for someone who preaches, the ability to use resource materials and commentaries and to examine the meaning of words by looking at the original Greek or Latin text is vital.

Incidentally, I don't believe it is necessary for a church leader to have gone to a Christian college, but he does need an education from a four-year liberal arts institution that has helped him to be a critical thinker, taught him how to use resources, and polished his abilities to write and speak.

I find it embarrassing to receive a letter from a man who calls himself a pastor or a minister but who communicates very poorly in written form, with multiple misspellings.

I believe the local church that ordains the ex-offender without adequate preparation may be unknowingly giving the ex-offender license in other areas without knowing it. Some ex-offenders I know struggle with pride. On occasion I have observed some who have set themselves up as equals with local pastors or prison chaplains because a local assembly has empowered them with an ordination.

I have witnessed the examination process toward ordination in several denominations. I am certainly well acquainted with the process in the Roman Catholic church, having accomplished seven years myself as a cleric. It is a rigorous route. It involves long and difficult study, research, and examination, all directed toward the same goal of insuring the credibility of the professional calling both to society and in the church. I think it appropriate for all churches to require equivalent standards from those who are called to lead them.

Strategy #7: Observe Basic Precautions

In addition to the precautions listed above, here are some basic guidelines for preventing con jobs and manipulations by ex-offenders. (These same precautions are listed concisely in Appendix D, under the heading "Practical and Professional Guidelines for Jail and Prison Ministry Volunteers.") Some of these precautions apply more specifically to professionals (chaplains) and volunteers actually working in prisons than to churches working in aftercare, but the basic principles are the same.

The primary difference is that church members cannot—and should not—keep the same distance from the unregenerated ex-offender who is a member of the church that they would keep from a prisoner who has not yet made a decision for Christ.

All of them would apply primarily to the first year or so after release, before the ex-offender has a chance to indicate by his behaviors whether his conversion is authentic and he is growing in Christ.

Do Not Run Errands for Inmates

One form of manipulation takes place when a prisoner or ex-offender gets the volunteer to do his work for him. A volunteer might consider a reasonable request, such as making one phone call, but errands should not become a pattern. One way to cultivate responsibility is to help the inmate solve his own problems. Many times family members can help, also, especially after release. There is a broad distinction between being helpful and becoming someone's chauffeur and errand boy.

Prison tends to make an inmate self-centered, even selfish. For this reason it is all the more important for the church to guide the ex-offender in responsible living.[3]

Do Not Get Involved in Business or Financial Transactions

To avoid the possibility of manipulation, it is a good idea for volunteers not to get directly involved with inmates' or ex-offenders' financial affairs. Here are some traps to avoid:

- co-signing an apartment lease for a prisoner awaiting release
- selling a car or other major possession for a prisoner

186

- getting involved in fundraising for a prisoner who operates an outside business or ministry

All of these can well be legitimate activities on the part of the inmate or ex-offender. And there may be times when a newly released ex-offender will need some form of financial help from a church. However, money and business are the areas in which the volunteer is most apt to be victimized by those intent on conning and manipulation.

Do Not Spend an Inordinate Amount of Time with One Inmate

This caution applies primarily to volunteers who work in a prison. These volunteers should remember they are not the prisoner's caseworker or private therapist. I once knew a volunteer who spent twenty hours a week visiting just one prisoner. This sent a message of favoritism to other prisoners. Such behavior also keeps the volunteer from sharing with a greater number of prisoners and increases the chances of developing a dependent relationship. Volunteers should keep in mind that their time with prisoners is a precious commodity, a resource that is always limited.

Chaplains Should Keep the Relationship Professional, Not Personal

While many volunteers can develop a meaningful friendship with a prisoner, and while churches should certainly focus on developing a personal relationship with an inmate, I believe that chaplains must maintain professional distance and boundaries.

The chaplain is really part of the administrative team of a corrections institution and must be able to make objective decisions that are free of personal bias and emotional involvement.

I once knew a chaplain whose close involvement with a prisoner led to a crime. The prisoner, a convicted child molester, asked the chaplain to deliver a note to a former victim, a twelve-year-old boy. The chaplain did so without opening the note. Unfortunately, the letter did not express repentance, as the chaplain had thought, but contained salacious material. The chaplain had come

187

to trust the inmate, but this relationship led him to suspend good judgment and common sense.

The event had ramifications for the offender's current trial, so the prosecutor's office was angry. In addition, because the chaplain had violated institutional policy, the sheriff removed his privilege of entering the facility. In the weeks that followed, the chaplain held interviews with local journalists, maintaining he had done nothing wrong. This embarrassed the sheriff, who succeeded in blocking future chaplains from coming into his institution as well. So this well-intentioned chaplain ended up setting the cause of Christ back for this particular institution—all because he made the mistake of transgressing professional boundaries with the prisoner.

Do Not Have Ex-Offenders Live with You or Your Relatives

This is a practical, commonsense recommendation. Church members can help the inmate by coordinating placement in a Christian halfway house or transitional living facility. Churches may even choose to subsidize an apartment or duplex where the ex-offender can live. Such strategies help the ex-offender begin the process of independent living while preventing potential problems that could arise when an ex-offender actually lives with a volunteer.

When I was a probation officer, a government policy forbade my taking any of my charges home. Sometimes I chafed against this policy. Often I would be responsible for a youngster who could not stay in his home because of neglect or abuse and no other facilities were available. I would have brought him home with me had this not been against the rules.

Looking back, however, I believe that policy was wise. Without it, many probation officers would probably have five or six people at a time living with them, and this would create conflicts with their jobs, especially when it came to reporting to the judge.

Many born-again believers who have been released from prison are stable and would make good neighbors and excellent house guests. But this is an area where manipulators are a reality and sociopaths can be dangerous. An ex-offender determined to play games can disrupt a marriage, create a perverse triangle in a relationship, and even create an incident that can result in violence. To avoid this kind of trouble, we must be cautious, truly "wise as serpents."

Do Not Have Ex-Offenders Work in Your Business for at Least One Year

This may seem contradictory to the idea of mentoring inmates and helping them develop a work ethic and job skills, but it really is not. I am speaking primarily to volunteers who own their own businesses. I would caution these men and women against taking newly released prisoners and employing them in their businesses—especially putting them behind cash registers or giving them access to financial books or sensitive files. Certainly the church should assist ex-offenders in finding gainful employment. But higher levels of responsibility should be progressive over time.

After one year, I believe it is reasonable to employ the ex-offender in a volunteer's business. Why a year? In my opinion, that is sufficient time to witness the ex-offender's growth in the local church and to observe behaviors that will show whether or not his conversion is authentic. The one-year waiting period simply prevents an ex-offender who is determined to manipulate the volunteer and then leave town from using the relationship for ulterior motives.

The ultimate ramifications of manipulation can be bad for the larger picture of ministry. The rip-off of a volunteer can create a bitter taste among others in the church and even dissuade them from involvement with prisoners. An ex-offender who steals from the McDonald's where he works has committed a crime, but his actions won't have nearly the impact on a church or a ministry that a crime against a volunteer would have.

Trust takes time to develop and build, and it cannot be rushed. I do advocate that Christian business people employ ex-offenders, but I believe it is reasonable to have a period of time to evaluate authenticity, especially if the employer is the volunteer who ministers to an inmate.

Do Not Lend Money

From Proverbs to Shakespeare and down to the present day, the advice holds true: Lending money is an unwise policy.

A prisoner may ask for money to buy commissary goods or to have money deposited to his account. This should be avoided. The more money or possessions an inmate has, the greater the potential for trouble ranging from extortion to gambling to bribery. Money and prison are a bad mixture.

Numerous articles are used in place of money in a prison. For instance, an inmate can play poker, gamble, or barter using cigarettes as money.

One common game inmates play with volunteers is to ask for stamps. The request is usually justified by the need to write to family, pen pals, or church people. But stamps also have monetary value and can be used as money inside the institution. Most institutions have a policy that prohibits visitors and volunteers from giving money or stamps to inmates. Even in the absence of such a policy, it is good to refrain from such activity.

We can help ex-offenders by providing opportunities, clothes, and food, but I would caution against giving newly released individuals expensive possessions or large sums of cash. One volunteer I know loaned his automobile to an ex-offender who then sold the car and used the money for drugs. The volunteer was not compensated.

Do Not Set Up a Speaking Circuit for Ex-Offenders

Although this has been explained in detail in chapter 5, a short recap might be in order. The newly released Christian needs to be nurtured and protected by the church. "Showing him off" or setting up a speaking circuit can be a form of exploitation; such activity can also hinder his growth by stoking his pride and ego or making it difficult for him to ask for help. Speaking about the "old days," even with an emphasis on conversion, can be a substitute for a real job. It may even be getting him in trouble. Several states have laws that restrict criminals from benefiting from their crimes. Such laws usually refer specifically to being paid to write a book or to having a screenplay written about an ex-offender's exploits, but they can also refer to making money by speaking.

At the very least, the local church should protect the ex-offender from overexposure during the first year after his release. If prominence does come, it should come through God's plan.

Keep Counseling and Visitation within Your Own Gender

This means that adult women should not work with adult male prisoners or ex-offenders—and vice versa. The possibilities of a sexual agenda or a romance developing are real, and this could lead to heartbreak or even danger if the prisoner is manipulative.

For similar reasons, I would not recommend that a female church member drive a male ex-offender without a third party present. The opposite would be true for a female ex-offender. Volunteers should confront words or behaviors that create discomfort, but not alone.

Remember, the ex-offender has most likely been in an environment of forced celibacy—an abnormal situation for any individual. If he is married, relationships at home may be strained. For these reasons, no matter how strong willed volunteers believe they are, it is just sound advice for men to mentor men and women to mentor women. In a counseling situation it is best not to mix genders.

Many female volunteers over the years have told me, "I am called to prison ministry." But when I recommend they go to a women's facility, some will insist, "No, no, God is only calling me to minister to the men!" That generally gives me cause for suspicion. Even though the volunteer may have the best of intentions and motives, she may also be responding to subconscious needs that make her vulnerable to being taken advantage of. It is possible for religious volunteers and church people to use "ministry" as an excuse for ulterior motives or simply bad judgment.

In one case, a young woman began living with a recently released prisoner who was not a believer. She did this "in the name of ministry," but it wasn't long before her lifestyle changed radically. Within a month, she was sexually involved with the ex-offender and had contracted a venereal disease. Soon she was riding on the back of a motorcycle and became involved with a violent urban gang. Why the sudden transformation? This young woman was sincere, but she was also lonely. She had few social contacts. I believe she sought prison ministry as an opportunity to meet her personal needs.

Now, I am not saying there is no place for women in prison ministry or working with male ex-offenders. Women can correspond with male prisoners and grade Bible studies. Certainly they can participate together in normal church activities. And of course they can visit women prisoners and incarcerated juveniles and serve as mentors for them when they get out of prison, yet I would recommend a mature woman. A female college freshman who is eighteen years old may be the same age as an incarcerated juvenile who is seventeen or eighteen. I would not recommend a mentoring relationship in this case.

Yes, there are exceptions to this rule. I have known Mother Consuella York for many years. She ministers to the tough men in the Cook County Jail. But not everyone is a Mother York! And she is always dressed appropriately, with a long black dress and a headpiece that resembles that of a nun. She serves as a mother figure and, in later years, a grandmother figure to these young inmates.

Watch for Dependency and Codependency

Chaplains, prison ministry volunteers, and churches working with ex-offenders need to maintain appropriate boundaries in their relationships with prisoners and ex-offenders. Certainly it is appropriate at times for volunteers to share some of their own life and problems with the inmate, but excessive sharing of one's own problems is inappropriate. The risk is that either the prisoner or the volunteer (or both) could become dependent on the relationship for consolation and friendship.

After release, one reason for cultivating responsibility and a strong work ethic in the ex-offender is to avoid his becoming unhealthily dependent on a ministry-cultivated relationship.

Make Sure Your Reputation Doesn't Hinge on an Inmate's Success

This advice is mostly for chaplains but also applies to the local church. Overexposing an ex-offender in the pulpit or in newsletters or touting the ex-offender's conversion as the proof of the ministry's effectiveness can lead to embarrassment and disappointment if there is backsliding or even major sin, including a return to crime. It is understandable to be proud of an ex-offender's progress, but the success of the ministry or of the chaplaincy should not hinge on any one inmate's story.

Work within Limits

Some volunteers and ministries find it difficult to avoid guilt when setting limits. Since God gives each volunteer specific gifts in ministry, it is important for volunteers not to feel they have to do it all. Some people are called to evangelism, some to discipleship, some to counseling, tutoring, helping with employment, housing, or church transition. Smaller prison ministries and certain individuals easily fall into the trap of believing they have to do it all. It is important to learn to network with other existing ministries and social services. Concentrate on doing one thing well!

Do Not Discuss Controversial Issues

A volunteer should never be in the position of arguing with a prisoner or ex-offender; there are far more constructive things to do with time. One way to avoid disputes is to stay off controversial subjects. The death penalty, for instance, is a subject that almost always arouses passion on both sides of the issue; it's best to stay away from it. Similarly, it's a good idea to avoid discussing correctional policy, how the warden runs the prison, political views, or minor theological differences. There are many topics of conversation about the biblical view of authority, forgiveness, spiritual freedom, resisting temptation, and dealing with anger and frustration that would be more productive.

Do Not Become Involved in the Legal Aspect of an Inmate's Case

Except in rare instances, I recommend that volunteers avoid becoming involved in the legal process. Do not campaign for early release. Do not write letters to the parole board. Do not write to the governor requesting clemency or the expungement of the ex-offender's record. Do not serve as a character witness. The only reasonable exception to this rule would be a case in which a volunteer has known the prisoner or the ex-offender for a long period of time and observed tremendous spiritual and emotional growth.

At any rate, common sense would dictate that the volunteer who is not a lawyer should refrain from discussing legal aspects of a case or giving legal advice to an inmate. Such involvement could lead to unwanted liability.

Do Not Give Details about Your Family

Reasonable precautions should be taken to avoid giving information a manipulative or sociopathic inmate can use to take advantage of a relationship with a volunteer. I always suggest that volunteers who correspond with inmates use a post-office box or the church address. College students should not give out their home addresses or their parents' occupations. Adult volunteers should not show photos of their children or give any details about their schools, family schedules, home addresses, or home phone numbers. These rules, of course, would apply to incarcerated inmates, not to ex-offenders. However, the transition to welcoming the newly released individual into church homes is predicated on a growing relationship during imprisonment. In this sense, the ex-offender is someone already known.

Seek Counsel When Uncomfortable

A volunteer who receives a letter from an inmate containing suggestive comments or sexual innuendo should immediately take the letter to his or her pastor or the leader of the prison ministry! The rule I generally give to volunteers is "Go with your intuition. If something the inmate does makes you uncomfortable, there is usually a good reason." This is also true after the inmate's release.

It is always best to involve church leadership when there is even a hint of inappropriate behavior. Vigilance in shepherding can avoid a lot of damage to the ex-offender, the church, or the ministry.

9

What Can the Church Do?

A Guide for Fostering Growth

The role of the church is fundamental to helping ex-offenders grow both emotionally and spiritually and helping to keep them from returning to crime. For many years, this truth has been clear to ministry leaders and volunteers who have worked in prison ministry. Until recently, however, there was little in the way of objective data to support the contention that the church really does make a difference in ex-offenders' lives.

After all, an ex-offender's statement that he is "happier," "doing better," or "feeling more peace" is good news, but it is also relative. What one ex-offender means by "feeling good" or "doing better" may mean something radically different from what another person means. I believe it is important to go beyond such subjective evidence of change to more objective, measurable standards. We need to adopt a standard of progress that presents convincing evidence to the nonbelieving world, including secular officials and government authorities, that the ministry of chaplains and church volunteers truly makes a difference in the lives of ex-offenders.

195

A 1990 article by Associated Press reporter George W. Cornell[1] reported the results of a study that verified the impact of religion (specifically Christianity) on prison recidivism.

John Gardner, a Baltimore clinical psychologist, headed a five-member research team that studied the effects of religion on prisoner rehabilitation. Gardner pointed out that "Researchers usually ignore religion. They look at all aspects of a person's life, but religion is a gap. It is a blind spot in the social sciences not even consistent with the spirit of science." According to Dr. Gardner the only previous study that showed the relationship between religion and prisoner rehabilitation had concerned transcendental meditation, not Christianity.

The research project studied 190 ex-offenders who took part between 1975 and 1979 in a Christian discipleship training program through Prison Fellowship. The research group then matched a control group of ex-offenders by gender, age, and race. The ex-offenders in both groups had been out of prison from between eight and fourteen years.

Among the study results were:

- Ex-offenders with an exposure to Christian discipleship in prison had an 11 percent lower recidivism rate than the control group.
- 41 percent of the Christian group committed new offenses, as compared to 51 percent of the control group.
- The recidivism rate for women with Christian discipleship in the prison was 19 percent lower than their control group.
- The Christian group remained crime free for a longer period after release.
- When Christians did commit new crimes, those crimes were less severe than those of the control group, whose crimes actually increased in severity.[2]

Gardner's study will of course need to be supplemented and verified by future studies. Nevertheless, the study is significant because it employed objective criteria to measure the influence of Christianity on inmates and ex-offenders. Proving and articulating these changes in a scientific way may well be able to open doors for volunteers and prison ministries to enter more institutions.

The Church As a Support System

Gardner's study focused on the recidivism effect of discipling inmates while they are still in prison. Preliminary research done by the Institute for Prison Ministries in 1989 suggests a similar effect of aftercare efforts on ex-offenders. This research demonstrates that inmates who come out of prison with a support system in place enjoy a 68–80 percent success record.

The more practical and spiritual support an ex-offender can claim in the period following his release, the more likely it is he will manage to stay out of prison and rebuild his life. Such support would include opportunities for employment, counseling, and education; a mentoring relationship; and shepherding from a local church.

I have long held the belief that a holistic approach to supporting and helping ex-offenders makes good sense. This diagram, which is based on Illinois's Life Skills Awareness Program (LEAP), provides a good model.[3]

A model for supporting ex-offenders, showing the components of a good support system.

197

The Right Church

I believe that membership in a local church is the linchpin in the Christian ex-offender's support system; it is vital for keeping the ex-offender growing and out of trouble. I recall an ex-offender who was having problems. I asked him how he was doing in his church, and he said, "I've been floating for some time. I've been shopping around for the right church." It did not surprise me that this ex-offender was having difficulties on several levels. I called his former pastor. The pastor said, "He drifts in and out. I really don't know him."

Individuals tend to seek churches they feel comfortable in, but comfort isn't the best reason for going to church. Tony Campolo once said during an address that "people go from church to church trying to get all their needs met. But the reason for going to church is to meet the needs of others."[4] I would add that the purpose for going to church is to know and be known by other Christians and to support one another in living for Christ.

It is important to teach ex-offenders what Dr. Campolo said so well. A man or woman who constantly moves from church to church each Sunday and never establishes roots has no chance to serve. He never gives a local congregation the opportunity to really know him and get into his life. He certainly doesn't develop the kind of support system that can help him grow and keep from falling back into crime.

Membership is more than signing on the dotted line. It means more than just showing up for a worship service once a week. Church membership, to me, means making a commitment to be involved with a specific congregation—attending services, taking advantage of Christian education, participating in ministry projects, enjoying fellowship. It means coming to know other members and being known by them. In such an environment, Christian growth becomes much easier.

A Christian Mentor

I am convinced that every Christian needs a spiritual mentor—but Christian prisoners and ex-offenders are in especial need of such one-on-one guidance. A mentoring relationship[5] is one in which an ex-offender is paired one-on-one with a church member who will provide ongoing emotional and spiritual support as well as practical help with the process of readjusting to society.

When I studied in a Benedictine monastery, the term for mentor was "spiritual director." Essentially this was a wiser and more mature Christian who could give recommendations in terms of prayer life, Bible study, and suggested devotional readings. A good mentor is a person who can handle confidences and can also serve as a dependable model.

Ideally, the process of mentoring the new believer should begin while the prisoner is still incarcerated. This is an important and sound aspect of growth for any Christian prisoner. The Match Two program of California is a great example of an effective mentoring program; it matches mature Christian adults with incarcerated juveniles and adults. Friends Outside, also of California, is another organization that matches adult volunteers with adult prisoners.

Once the prisoner is released, I am convinced that a trusting mentoring relationship is the most effective tool for helping that ex-offender grow in Christ and stay away from crime. Such a relationship takes time to build. A mentor from a local church must win the right to be heard and must work to become a significant person in the ex-offender's life. Mentors will need to meet regularly with the offenders, be alert for special needs (such as job training or marital counseling), pray with them, and confront them if necessary.

There are several words we can use synonymously with a mentoring model. It is a discipleship program. It is a kind of apprenticeship. It is a way of modeling good behavior and character. Most basically, however, it is a *friendship*. More than any other relationship, an ex-offender needs a friend. He needs someone who will provide support and encouragement but who will also hold him accountable and correct him in love. He needs someone who will serve as an example of spiritual maturity.

If every Christian ex-offender had a mentor in a local church, I am convinced the success rate of ex-offenders would be phenomenal! J. Michael Quinlan,[6] former director of the Federal Bureau of Prisons, echoes that sentiment: "A mentoring relationship is fundamental to keep prisoners from returning to crime."

Who should be a mentor? No special skills or background are necessary for this important task, but Christian maturity is a must. I also believe that the mentor should be of the same gender as the ex-offender; this would preclude the possibility of romantic infatuation or even sexual involvement developing between mentor and ex-offender.

Churches might want to consider using retired people as a mighty army in a mentoring program. With early retirement more common, more and more people in their early or middle sixties find themselves with time to spare, ample energy, and a desire to become involved. Couple with that the fact that many of the older people in our congregations have served in positions of leadership as deacons and elders; some have even come back from missionary fields. These are people with a vast reservoir of spiritual maturity—precisely the kinds of people who could serve as appropriate Christian models for growing, Christian ex-offenders.[7]

Persistent Shepherding

The need for shepherding is part of the ongoing pastoral duty conferred on Christian leaders in the Scriptures. The guidance shepherding provides holds each church member accountable for his or her behaviors. In this respect, the ex-offender is no different from any other member of the church. It is true that the ex-offender has an identified criminal background and specific past habits and tendencies, but all members have weaknesses and tendencies that may call for shepherding.

Shepherding is much more than keeping a watch out for potential sin. It is a tender, loving relationship in which church leadership remains close to those in their flock, looking for signs of trouble and gently guiding them toward sources of healing.

A prisoner at Leavenworth penitentiary once said to me, "I attended church before I came to prison. I went back to church and again went to prison. No one got into my life. No one really took the time to find out what was happening."

Those words struck me as an indictment of the church. Someone was shirking his shepherding responsibility.

Having an ex-offender in your church means so much more than a polite handshaking after the service. Church leaders must take the time truly to shepherd the ex-offender, keeping track of his needs and his struggles and leading him gently in the direction he needs to go. Leaders cannot afford to wait for an urgent phone call. In the first few months, when he is most vulnerable, they need to initiate contact—call him, drop over to his residence, invite him out for dinner. Taking the time to listen is especially important. Church members should ask, "How are you feeling?" "Have you had any periods of loneliness or sadness?" "Do you miss your family?" "Is there something I can do?"

Granted, the answers to these questions will depend on the level of trust that has been built. But regardless of the answers, church leaders must keep on initiating communication, repeatedly reminding the ex-offender that the doors of a relationship are open to him. I believe nothing is more important to the ex-offender's ongoing growth than the combination of a one-on-one mentoring relationship and careful shepherding by church leaders. It is the church's responsibility to do this and, in my estimation, the church is the best equipped to fulfill this role. The ultimate goal of this shepherding is to equip the ex-offender both for independent living and for an active and vital role in the local church.

One of the most important things a shepherd can do in an ex-offender's life is to get him involved in Bible studies. Church leaders and mentors should not simply accept his word that he is reading his Bible everyday, but should actually study the Bible with him. If he is a spiritual "baby"—or even if he has grown past that stage—Scripture is the nourishment he will need to move toward greater levels of spiritual maturity.

A Support Hot Line

Jim Wilson, Network Specialist with Illinois's Life Skills Employment Awareness Program recently shared with me an excellent idea for ministering to ex-offenders that could supplement the mentoring and shepherding activities in the local church and help take care of ex-offenders that "slip through the cracks."

Jim recommends a crisis line for ex-offenders, an 800 number that would be staffed twenty-four hours a day, seven days a week, by local churches. (He suggested dubbing the number, 1–800-STAY-OUT.) The person answering the phone at such a service would be trained and would have access to a computer database that would list resources both in social services and in churches by region.

This is a marvelous idea for a role the church could play in stabilizing a newly released Christian ex-offender. Implementing it would take special people who are willing to be called late at night. But the rewards could be tremendous.

When Jim spoke to a group of ex-offenders recently, he asked them how often they had been to prison. At least 60 percent had been to prison more than twice—a typical pattern. Then Jim posed this question, "If you had a friend you could have called before you committed a new crime, would you have gone back to prison?" The overwhelming response was that if they had had someone to call at the moment of desperation, they probably would not have committed the crime.

What kind of calls would be typical?

- A man is kicked out of a local YMCA and needs a place to sleep.
- An ex-offender is at the end of his rope and needs to talk to someone.
- A woman needs a referral for medical care.

Several months ago I received a phone call from a man named Steve. He was calling from the East Coast. I did not recognize the mature husky voice. Suddenly, I realized whom I was talking to. I had been Steve's probation officer nearly fourteen years before, when he was fifteen years old.

Steve said he was desperate. He had been unemployed for several months and was thinking of robbing a 7–11 store. Basically, he wanted me to talk him out of it.

My first thoughts went back to those years when Steve was a juvenile delinquent. We had not gotten along well. His criminal behavior had escalated, and eventually I had recommended that he be sent to the Department of Corrections. In fact, I had testified against him in court.

So why was Steve calling me after so many years?

I suppose I have omitted a significant part of the story. One month after he was sent to the Department of Corrections, I had visited Steve at the institution where he was locked up. Perplexed, he had asked me why I had come. He had thought I hated him. I had answered that I did not think prison was good for him but his ongoing behavior had left no choices to the court and the community. Somehow I must have gotten across the message that, despite our rough times, I really did care about him. Now after many years, without family or friends and in a desperate position, he started wondering if anyone out there cared—and my name came to his mind.

This is the real value of a mentoring program. When we really get into someone's life and build trust, the ex-offender is given a foundation and a support that he can lean on.

A Practical Agenda

A correctional officer at California's San Quentin prison told me recently, "On an average, seven men get released each day. We let them out of the west gate and point them down the road to the bus station, a half mile away. Years ago," he continued, "we used to say good luck to each man leaving. Today we say, 'See you again!'"

I do not believe the correctional officer was being overly cynical. What he said was based in reality. Sending a man down the highway with a hundred-dollar check (part of which must be used for a bus ticket) and no family, church, or support system is just setting him up for failure.

General William Booth, the founder of the Salvation Army, understood the need to address the practical needs of hurting people as well as meeting their spiritual needs. Consistent with the gospel mandate found in Matthew 25, the Book of James, and Hebrews, we need to feed hungry people before we preach to them. Ex-offenders have many practical needs, including:

A New Neighborhood or Town

I am convinced it is important for an ex-offender to get out of his old neighborhood and find a new place to live. One of the greatest factors that leads to failure is getting back with old friends and being exposed to old addictions—gambling, drugs, drinking, sex, violence, and gang activity.

This need for a new location is so great that, in my opinion, it even takes precedence over cross-cultural issues. It is far better to take an African-American and transplant him into a white sub-urb, for instance, than to send him back to an old environment with all the temptations for crime and instant gratification.

If the ex-offender has gotten to know volunteers from a partic-ular church while in prison, it makes sense that he would relocate to the community where that church is located. Church members could provide transportation from prison to the new neighbor-hood, help locate a room or an apartment, arrange for utilities and other services, offer maps and "get acquainted" tours, and invite the ex-offender over for meals and do what is necessary to help him feel at home.

Transportation

From day one, a released man needs transportation—first to the town where he will reside, and then from place to place within the town.

The ex-offender may need help getting a driver's license. Even if he already knows how to drive, a brush-up course to make him aware of any changes in the law would be helpful. Something as simple as driving him to the testing area and being with him would be a great encouragement. And the donation of a car may also be a lifesaver, especially in areas where public transportation is unavailable, unreliable, or very expensive.

Often a church member will have a second or third car—a "beater"—that he or she would gladly donate to an ex-offender. It goes without saying that the auto should be reliable and drivable.

Housing

An ex-offender in a new community will certainly need a place to live. A halfway house or a transitional living facility can be especially helpful in smoothing the transition into free society. If no such facility is available, the ex-offender will need a place to stay—even if it is just a bedroom in the back of someone's home.

I am not advocating handouts here. The ex-offender should be required to pay rent, although a church or network might choose to subsidize the housing until the ex-offender can get back on his feet.

Social Services

The church can also be instrumental in linking the ex-offender with existing social services in the community. The ex-offender may need food stamps, for instance, while he is getting on his feet, or he may need access to low-cost medical and dental care.

Household Basics

Just as a young engaged couple are given a "shower" to furnish them with basic household necessities, so would an ex-offender benefit from the donation of such items. The ex-offender will need just about everything, including:

- a bed
- a table and chairs
- dishes, flatware, and cooking utensils
- bed linens
- towels
- a lamp
- a small couch or sofa
- simple tools

These could be provided through donations by church members or by a "shopping trip" to thrift stores and garage sales. Or the church could give the ex-offender a shower of his own to provide him with the basics.

205

In addition, the ex-offender will need clothes and pantry staples. Many churches already maintain a pantry or closet for this purpose. The donation of warm clothing is especially important in Midwestern or Northeastern areas; a man who has been in prison for ten years is not prepared for a cold winter.

A Survival Kit

I recently learned of a Chicago attorney who has introduced a concept now being used by several prison ministries and churches in the state of Illinois. The attorney recommended giving every released Christian ex-offender a survival kit—a large simulated-leather bag that contains important supplies for the first few months. I recently examined such a bag and discovered the following contents:

- one alarm clock
- one calendar
- three pairs of underwear
- three T-shirts
- three pairs of socks
- one set of work gloves
- a New Testament
- ten envelopes with stamps and pen
- several motivational booklets
- a map of the city
- a map of bus routes
- a community service directory
- a large tube of toothpaste
- a can of deodorant
- a bottle of shampoo
- six bars of soap
- a can of shaving cream
- a razor

The bag I examined had been made by inmates in the Prison Industries in Menard State Prison in Illinois. The quality was very good, and because of the relatively low cost of prison labor, the bag cost a total of $7.60. The value of the contents of the survival kit totaled $22.68. For slightly over $30, in other words, an ex-offender could be supplied with basic necessities that can make all the difference during the first days and the first weeks of his freedom.

What an excellent idea! Giving each man coming into a community a survival kit is not merely an expression of caring; it can also be a practical godsend during the period after release.

And the cost could be brought down considerably. Businessmen from a church could make donations of various products. Also it would be in the best interest of retail stores to make contributions. A ministry or church could solicit a cotton mill to donate irregular T-shirts as contributions. A large chain such as K-Mart could contribute cartons of soap, deodorant, or toothpaste from their overstock.

Help with Practical Skills

The ex-offender may experience contradictory feelings. He may be experiencing the exhilaration of freedom. At the same time, his freedom can seem overwhelming because he either has lost or never developed some basic skills for living on the outside. Church volunteers who donate their time to help the ex-offender acquire these skills can make a significant contribution.

For instance, an ex-offender who has been dependent on an institution for many years probably needs to learn basic domestic skills. Even if he has taken a turn as a cook in the prison, he has been used to preparing meals in massive quantities and may not have the skills to cook in smaller quantities. He may also need help in learning to read labels, shop for bargains, and use leftovers.

Another important area where an ex-offender may need special tutoring would be sharpening his communication skills. This would include helping to expand his vocabulary, write letters, fill out job applications, and interpret forms and contracts. At a more basic level, he may need help learning to read.

Financial skills are absolutely crucial to whether the inmate will make a successful transition to free society. Church members can help the ex-offender learn how to balance a checkbook, set up a budget, and begin to save for the future while at the same time tithing to the local church and making restitution to victims. The ex-offender may also need guidance in avoiding a spirit of materialism.[8]

Ongoing Education

Most ex-offenders know that an education goes a long way toward increasing their chances of survival and stability. The average inmate in America functions at a fourth- or fifth-grade reading level and dropped out of school by the ninth or tenth grade. This of course reduces an ex-offender's chances of getting a good job.

Many inmates acquire a General Education Diploma (GED) or high-school equivalency while in prison. But for those who do not—or those who need even more basic literacy training—the church can play a vital role. Linking an ex-offender with a literacy or GED program at a local community college or school system is helpful.

For ex-offenders who are ready for college, the Charles W. Colson scholarship program at Wheaton College, Wheaton, Illinois, offers an opportunity for further education. As mentioned previously, I have the great privilege of administering this program. As I write, eleven ex-offenders have completed the program with both four-year bachelor of arts degrees and master's degrees. Several are currently enrolled in the program. For more information on the program, write to Institute for Prison Ministries, Attention: Ex-Offender Scholarships, Billy Graham Center, Wheaton, Illinois, 60187.

Higher education is a worthy investment a church can make in an ex-offender's life. Individual churches can assist ex-offenders with tuition subsidies, scholarship programs, or other forms of support. For instance, small churches might not be able to pay the tuition of a college education, but they may be able to help with the many supplemental costs, including transportation to the college, resettling the ex-offender's family, and food and clothing. Help with any of these expenses would reduce the stress that an ex-offender returning to college is likely to experience.

Additional Tips for Helping Ex-Offenders

There are several additional practical tips for how church people can help ex-offenders become functioning members of free society:

Get Involved with the Prisoner before He Is Released

The best time to begin the relationship with an ex-offender is before he is an ex-offender! Churches need to build relational bridges to prisoners before release. A one-on-one visitation ministry to a local jail or prison will build the kind of relationships that make reentry into the community and the local church much easier. The natural outgrowth of such relationships would be for the volunteer to invite the prisoner to his or her church.[9]

Visitation is not the same thing as evangelism; it is more of a prerequisite. Evangelism develops naturally from a trusting relationship. The Scriptures (Matt. 25 and Heb. 13) tell us to visit prisoners. Basically, this means being a friend by listening, encouraging, and comforting.

Prisoners will want to attend a church if church members have been consistent in supporting them while they were incarcerated. And visitation is not the only form of support. Those who are unable to visit—the elderly and shut-ins, for example—can be very effective encouragers through a pen-pal program. In fact, this may have a greater impact in some instances than a visit, because prisoners will read and reread a letter. I know prisoners who have accepted Christ through a series of letters from a devoted Christian.

As I said before, I believe we should keep this visitation mentoring within the same gender; males should visit males and females should visit females. The only exception to this, in my opinion, is with a male juvenile population. In this case, an older, mature woman could provide a motherly influence.

Do Not Do Everything for the Ex-Offender

Even though I have previously outlined some of the areas in which churches and individuals can help ex-offenders get started, it is important to remember that the ultimate goal is to help the individual become responsible for himself, not to do everything for him. It is okay for church members to say no to ex-offenders' requests. Church members do not have to become chauffeurs or servants, responding to every request for assistance. Over the long haul, I believe that most ex-offenders want to move out of dependence to a stage of healthy interdependence. Churches involved in ministry to ex-offenders should help them move toward that goal.

A Chicago judge recently said, "If we really want to punish crime in America, we should make every offender get up at 6:00 A.M., drive in traffic jams, sit behind a desk for endless hours, then have a large chunk of his paycheck go to taxes . . . make him live like everyone else!" He was describing not only a work ethic, but being cynical about how everyday life is harder than the daily routine of some prisoners. Churches that help build responsibility in ex-offenders are making a great contribution.

Get the Ex-Offender Involved in a Range of Activities

The goal for helping an ex-offender adjust to the outside world is to help him become a normal citizen. Churches can help him work toward this goal by involving him in a number of different activities—work, certainly, but also wholesome leisure activities. Church members can invite ex-offenders to play miniature golf or go to a movie or concert. They can take him sightseeing in a nearby city or explore different ethnic restaurants. Certainly, they should invite him over for dinner.

These activities do not need to be specifically church-related; in fact, it's better if they are not. If all the activities center around the church, the ex-offender will simply have been transferred from the isolated environment of the prison to the insulated environment of the church.

The church is located in the larger community, and the ex-offender must learn to resist the temptations that are out there for everyone. If he should stumble—say, pick up a pornographic magazine or drink too much at a bar one night—a caring church and a mentor-friend can help him get back on track. But if he is tethered to the church the way some parents have a leash attached to the wrist of a toddler, the ex-offender will really not have opportunities to grow emotionally and spiritually.

Do Not Judge All Ex-Offenders from a Previous Bad Experience

If your church is actively involved in prison ministry and working with ex-offenders, chances are that you will eventually be manipulated or conned in some way. I would urge you not to let this bad experience keep you from working with ex-offenders. Start anew with each person, heeding the scriptural admonition to be "wise as serpents," but also judging him on his behavior as an individual and not on the behavior of someone else. Proverbs 28:13 (LB) reminds us, "A man who refuses to admit his mistakes can never be successful. But if he confesses and forsakes them, he gets another chance."

To keep from dwelling on an experience with a manipulative ex-offender, churches have only to remember that manipulation or mistreatment of others is not just an ex-offender trait! Most of us know what it's like to be disappointed by friends, gossiped about by someone we trusted, or even betrayed by someone in our own church. The same thing can happen with ex-offenders, but it won't *always* happen with ex-offenders.

Do Not Set the Ex-Offender on a Pedestal

As discussed in chapter 5, the church needs to protect the newly released ex-offender from too much notoriety and responsibility, even though the ex-offender's hunger for attention may drive him to seek the spotlight.

A Christian ex-offender just out of prison should not be overly used as a speaker or exposed on a speaking circuit. Although some churches mean well, they tend to show off the ex-offender as a trophy of God's grace. That only puts greater pressure on the ex-offender to look and act perfect, which he surely is not.

Maintain Realistic Expectations

Don't be shocked if the ex-offender backslides in minor or even major ways. Major lifestyle changes are rarely made without some backward movement.

211

Church members should not be shocked if a profane word falls from the ex-offender's lips at one time or another. Remember, he has heard profanity day in and day out in the prison, and before his conversion he may have used it extensively. The words are still in his brain and may come out unpredictably.

The ex-offender's time on the outside will likely begin with a sort of honeymoon period, when he will be on his best behavior. Then, once he begins to realize he has a multitude of choices, the ex-offender may go through many phases of feeling and behavior: resistance to authority, expressions of formerly repressed anger, spiritual dryness, and ambivalence about the church. This is to be expected and should be handled with patience and understanding. Above all, it's important not to give up on him if he sins or fails!

That doesn't mean that churches who are working with ex-offenders should put up with clearly wrong behavior such as lying, stealing, or other forms of manipulation. On the contrary, the church is the proper place for discipline, and attention to these matters should be swift and certain. But discipline should not mean harshness or desertion. It's possible to affirm and love someone while disciplining them. Church members who think an ex-offender is exaggerating, lying, or conning them should call him on it—immediately—but always do so in love.

An ex-offender who gets away with manipulation will lose respect for the person he is conning, and he is also more likely to fall into more manipulative behavior, thus increasing his chances of a new offense. Holding up a mirror to bad habits may hurt at first, but in the long run it will show the church's commitment to his growth.

Help the Ex-Offender Develop a Servant Spirit

I am convinced that an ex-offender begins to grow to the degree that he becomes a servant.

Many years ago, I lived in a monastic setting while studying graduate-level theology. From a wonderful Benedictine priest I learned a practical example of the servant attitude. During a monastic meal, food was put in the center of the table, family style. The monks were not allowed to take any food or water for themselves. Instead, they were to observe the plates and cups of the brothers who were sitting to their right and left. If a brother's cup was empty, the monk would reach for the pitcher and pour more water without waiting to be asked. If a man was thirsty or hungry, it was because someone had not watched out for him—because his neighbors were thinking only about themselves.

What a marvelous example of servanthood! If we in the church are watching out for the needs of other people, our focus will be off of ourselves. This is the kind of servant mindset that Paul describes in 2 Corinthians 1:4, that "we can comfort those in any trouble with the comfort we ourselves have received from God." And this servant mindset is what we want to develop in the ex-offender.

The ex-offender has a servanthood advantage when it comes to helping hurting people. He himself was formerly broken-hearted. Out of that weakness, he has a great opportunity to be a blessing to others. The ex-offender will always know what it feels like to be rejected. He also has a key sensitivity to the needs of new ex-offenders and their families coming into the community and the local church. The growing ex-offender is thus a marvelous resource in the local church for reaching out to other hurting people in the community.

Above All, Be Patient

Church people represent normal people. Prisoners, though, have been living in a very abnormal culture. A newly released ex-offender's initial paranoia may be real. He may even suspect the church's motives at times. Because the basic posture of an ex-offender while in prison was "always watch your back," he may be overly defensive. A cynical or manipulative ex-offender is likely to consider church people "squares."

Sitting in church on a Sunday morning, the ex-offender may feel sure that everybody is looking at him. He may enter a restaurant and believe that a cop who is sitting there knows about his background. He may suspect the neighbors know his past.

It's important to keep holding the ex-offender accountable for his behavior. He should not be allowed to treat members of the congregation like parole officers—giving minimal answers and

213

always insisting that everything is "fine." (A prisoner who says that consistently is either hiding something or out of touch with himself.) At the same time, it's important not to push too hard. It's better to be patient and let trust develop gradually.

Because the inmate may struggle with feelings of mistrust and even paranoia, the church should not overemphasize the ex-offender's background. I recall a church that would always introduce the ex-offender by saying, "This is Tim Brown; he was in prison for murder, but now he is a Christian." The ex-offender would smile politely, but this introduction made it hard for him to shake his old negative label. If he felt on a Sunday morning that everybody was looking at him, he was probably correct!

An ex-offender's background is really a confidential matter; he should be allowed to share it only when he feels comfortable. I know many ex-offenders who have gone ten or twenty years without ever telling anyone outside a select group about their background. That must be the individual's decision, and the church must respect that.

Helping Ex-Offenders Grow

There is no easy way to grow.[10] There is no simple book with ten easy steps to make us into spiritual giants. Growing in Christ is a slow process for all Christians, not just ex-offenders. All of us know what it is like to make progress and then backslide. For the ex-offender, the road to growth may be harder to travel because of his load of emotional baggage and his habit of playing games. But the church is in a unique position to help him along that road.

How can a local church help an ex-offender grow?

- We can *support* the ex-offender while holding him accountable.
- We can provide *practical help* without constant handouts.[11]
- We can adopt a *tough-love* stance, trusting but not allowing ourselves be manipulated.
- We can *be proud of* an ex-offender's transformation without putting him in a spotlight or up on a pedestal.

214

- We can *affirm* an ex-offender's spiritual growth by observing behaviors and not falling for words and jargon alone.
- We can *forgive* an ex-offender's sin[12] or manipulation and yet still exercise discipline.
- We can *provide structure*, limits, and guidelines for men and women who may have never had balanced parental authority in their lives—thus teaching them to handle authority appropriately.
- We can *be patient*, remembering, as ex-offender Manny Mill once said to me, that "the ex-offender begins from zero."
- Above all, we can continue to *reach out in love*, rejoicing in the power of God to bring the most unlikely men and women into his kingdom!

*A*ppendix A

Prison Ministries

The following national prison ministries have actively developed their aftercare resources.

Bill Glass Prison Ministry
P.O. Box 1105
Cedar Hill, TX 75104
214-291-7895

For more than twenty years, this ministry has been on the frontline of evangelism in prisons across America. They have also developed a follow-up strategy which they use in local communities, working with Campus Crusade.

The Bridge
2100 Brengle Avenue
Orlando, FL 32808
407-291-1500

Frank Costantino, the president of the Coalition of Prison Evangelists, also administers two halfway houses for ex-offenders in the state of Florida. The original home in Orlando is called "The Bridge." His working partnership with state government provides an excellent model. Hundreds of male and female ex-offenders have gone through his program since 1976.

Good News Jail and Prison Ministry
9401 Mathy Drive, Suite 100
Fairfax, VA 22031
703-764-2001

The Good News chaplains in more than 130 jails across the nation maintain close ties to the local church. Their President's Council calls together pastors and local leaders from the community who support the chaplain and who help the ex-offender in the aftercare phase. In addition, Good News Bible Correspondence courses are of excellent quality and prepare the ex-offender for his release through increased spiritual maturity.

Match-Two Prisoner Outreach

Box 447
San Quentin, CA 94964
415-457-8701

This program coordinates one-on-one matches in adult and juvenile institutions of California, with Match-Two Job Therapy divisions in Washington, Nevada, and Wisconsin. Match-Two has tremendous expertise in recruiting, screening, and monitoring volunteers. They are also in the process of developing aftercare strategies.

Prison Fellowship

P.O. Box 17500
Washington, DC 20041
703-478-0100

This widely known prison ministry is active in three areas of aftercare:

1. Life Plan Seminars: These two- to three-day seminars help prisoners develop realistic goals and practical skills, including finding a job and managing finances.

2. Mentoring: Prison Fellowship coordinates a one-on-one mentoring relationship between the volunteer and prisoner. After release, the volunteer meets the prisoner each week for six months to give encouragement and provide a strong Christian model.

3. Philemon Fellowship: This support group consists of ex-prisoners and their families and features spiritual encouragement and biblical teaching.

Salvation Army (Correctional Division)

615 Slaters Lane
P.O. Box 269
Alexandria, VA 22313
703-684-5500

In most major cities, the Salvation Army runs halfway houses that can accommodate ex-offenders. Some have strict guidelines that include guidance and biblical teaching, but they have proved very effective in stabilizing released offenders.

Teen Challenge

1445 Boonville Avenue
Springfield, MO 65802
417-862-2781

This is one of the most effective organizations working with juvenile delinquents who have drug or alcohol dependencies. Biblical teaching is coupled with the drug education and emotional support.

Yokefellows

1200 Almond Street
Williamsport, PA 17701
717-326-6868

This organization has been active in jails and prisons since 1968. They have developed specific plans for aiding the re-entry of offenders into the community. They also work closely with local churches in building bridges to individuals about to be released.

*A*ppendix B

Churches Ministering in Jails and Prisons

The following list of churches involved in prison ministry was compiled by the Institute for Prison Ministries in March and April of 1992. Church names were submitted by key prison-ministry leaders across the nation.

This list is intended as a resource for church leaders who wish to become involved in jail and prison ministry. It is *not* to be used as a donor list or mailing list for the solicitation of support!

East

Bethel Gospel Assembly
2-26 E. 120th Street
New York, NY 10035
212-369-8066

Calvary Baptist
123 W. 57th Street
New York, NY 10019
212-975-0170

Calvary Church
1401 Espenshade Road
Lancaster, PA 17601
717-394-3768

Fairton Christian Center
P.O. Box 96
Fairton, NJ 08320
609-455-5783

Forcey Memorial Church
2130 East Randolph Road
Silver Spring, MD 20904
301-622-2200

Maranatha Baptist Church
Route 1, Box 240
Bridgeton Pike
Millville, NJ 08332
609-455-8818

New Hope Baptist Church
37 Schafer Avenue
Cedarville, NJ 08311
609-447-3024

Webster Bible Church
675 Holt Road
Webster, NY 1450
716-872-5150

Zion Baptist Church
Camden, NJ 08101
609-541-4448

Zion Hill Baptist Church
841 Shepherd Street, N.W.
Washington, DC 20011
202-722-1580

South

Barcroft Bible Church
P.O. Box 2726
Fairfax, VA 22031
703-591-6900

Brownsville Baptist Church
2601 W. Strong Street
Pensacola, FL 32505
904-435-8287

Calvary Assembly
1199 Clay Street
Winter Park, FL 32792
407-644-1199

Calvary Baptist Church
1505 Broad Street
Bristol, TN 37620
615-968-5919

Calvary Evangel Baptist Church
205 Gust Lane
Portsmouth, VA 23701
804-485-3658

Cherrydale Baptist Church
3910 Lorcum Lane
Arlington, VA 22207
703-525-8210

Downtown Baptist Church
212 South Washington Street
Alexandria, VA 22314
703-549-5544

First Baptist Church
500 N. Palafax Street
Pensacola, FL 32501
904-433-5631

Harlan Park Baptist Church
1895 Highway 286 West
Conway, AR 72302
214-228-1281

Immanuel Baptist Church
3601 Monument Avenue
Richmond, VA 23230
804-355-8691

Orlando Community Church
816 Broadway Avenue
Orlando, FL 32803
407-841-8999

Midwest

Christ Way Baptist Church
1210 E. 62nd Street
Chicago, IL 60637
312-363-9563

Elmbrook Church
777 S. Barker Road
Waukesha, WI 53186
414-786-7051

First Christian Reformed Church
16248 South Park Avenue
South Holland, IL 60373
708-333-8211

The Gospel House
14707 Alexander Road
Walton Hills, OH
216-439-6655

Great Commission Baptist Church
23441 W. 8 Mile Road
Detroit, MI 48219
313-255-7995

Harmony Heights Baptist Church
P.O. Box 2008
Joplin, MO 64803
417-781-1700

Minnetonka Baptist Church
4420 Highway 1010 South
Minnetonka, MN 55345
612-474-0858

North Heights Lutheran Church
2701 N. Rice Street
Roseville, MN 55113
612-484-2049

Trinity Baptist Church
25W741 Jewel Road
Wheaton, IL 60187
708-653-8400

Ward Presbyterian Church
1700 Farmington
Livonia, MI 48154
313-422-1150

Westbrook Evangelical Free Church
1920 Robertson Drive
Omaha, NE 68104
402-397-9407

Willow Creek Community Church
67 E. Algonquin Road
South Barrington, IL 60010
708-765-5000

Xenos Christian Fellowship
611 E. Weber Road
Columbus, OH 43211
614-262-3275

Southwest

Council Road Baptist Church
2900 N. Council
Bethany, OK 73008
405-789-3175

Oak Cliff Bible Fellowship
1808 W. Camp Wisdom Road
Dallas, TX 75232
214-228-1281

Phoenix First Assembly of God
13613 N. Cave Creek Road
Phoenix, AZ 85022
602-867-7117

Prestonwood Baptist Church
15720 Hillcrest
Dallas, TX 75248
214-387-4475

West Coast

Calvary Chapel
27462 Enterprise Circle West
Temecula, CA 92590
714-699-0553

Capitol Christian Center
9470 Micron Avenue
Sacramento, CA 95827
916-363-5683

Crenshaw Christian Center
7901 S. Vermont
Los Angeles, CA 90044
213-565-4194

Evangelical Free Church
P.O. Box 786
Yorba Linda, CA 92686
714-524-1744

Fair Haven Bible Chapel
401 McArthur Boulevard
San Leandro, CA 94577
510-568-2488

First Christian Reformed Church
2175 Leoni Drive
Hanford, CA 93230
209-582-4423

Harvest Christian Fellowship
6115 Arlington Avenue
Riverside, CA 92504
714-687-6902

Loveland Baptist Church
2654 West Foothill Boulevard
San Bernardino, CA 92410
714-829-0777

North Hollywood Assembly of God
11455 Burbank Boulevard
North Hollywood, CA 91601
818-766-4341

People's Church
P.O. Box 17879
Salem, OR 97305
503-393-1613

People's Church
7172 N. Cedar
Fresno, CA 93720
209-298-8001

San Francisco Christian Center
5828 Mission Street
San Francisco, CA 94112
415-584-5515

Vaca Valley Christian Life Center
6391 Leisure Town Road
Vacaville, CA 95687
707-448-3124

West Adams Four Square Church
2614 S. LaBrea Avenue
Los Angeles, CA 90016
213-937-6128

Appendix C

Correspondence Courses

American Bible Academy
P.O. Box 1490
Joplin, MO 64802
417-781-9100

*Columbia Bible College and
Extension Studies*
Box 3122
Columbia, SC 29230-3122
803-754-4100

*Emmaus Correspondence School
(30 branch offices across country)*
2570 Asbury Road
Dubuque, IA 52001
319-588-8000

*Institute for Correspondence
Studies*
Summit Christian College
1025 West Rudisill Boulevard
Ft. Wayne, IN 46807
219-456-2111

Liberty University
Box 20000
Lynchburg, VA 24506-80001
804-522-4700

*Moody Bible Institute/Center for
External Studies*
820 N. LaSalle
Chicago, IL 60610-3284
312-329-4000

National Home Study Council
1601 Eighteenth Street, N.W.
Washington, DC 20009
202-234-5100

Trinity College
2077 Half Day Road
Deerfield, IL 60015
708-948-8980

Washington Bible College
6511 Princess Garden Parkway
Lanham, MD 20706
301-552-1400

*Western Conservative Baptist
Seminary*
5511 S.E. Hawthorne Boulevard
Portland, OR 97215
503-233-8561

*A*ppendix D

Practical and Professional Guidelines for Jail and Prison Ministry Volunteers

1. Do not run errands for inmates.
2. Do not get involved in business or financial transactions.
3. Do not spend an inordinate amount of time with one inmate.
4. Chaplains should keep the relationship professional, not personal.
5. Do not have ex-offenders live with you or your relatives.
6. Do not have ex-offenders work in your business for at least one year.
7. Do not lend money.
8. Do not set up a speaking circuit for the ex-offender.
9. Keep counseling and visitation within your own gender.
10. Watch for dependency or co-dependency.
11. Make sure your reputation doesn't hinge on an inmate's success.
12. Work within limits.
13. Do not discuss controversial issues, for example the death penalty.
14. Do not become involved in the legal aspect of an inmate's case.
15. Do not give details about your family.
16. Seek counsel when uncomfortable.

*N*otes

Introduction

1. Statistics in this introduction were provided by a telephone interview with an information officer at the Bureau of Justice Statistics, a division of the U.S. Department of Justice. They maintain a databank of current statistics regarding crime and federal corrections. For additional information see: Kathleen Maguire, Editor, *Sourcebook of Criminal Justice Statistics 1992*, Washington D.C.: U.S. Department of Justice, 1993.

2. In 1989 Zondra Linblade and Dwayne Elmer of Wheaton College completed a survey of prison ministries in America that had been commissioned and published in 1990 by the Institute for Prison Ministries Billy Graham Center. The method of this survey was a random sampling of a comprehensive list of five hundred prison ministries. There was a 71 percent response with a margin of error of plus or minus 3 percent.

3. The program began in 1986 and has ten graduates.

4. In their comprehensive book, *Criminology, Crime and Criminality* (New York: Houghton Mifflin, 1983), authors Martin R. Haskell and Lewis Yablonski discuss the effects of imprisonment, stating, "Prisoners tend to be weak and emotionally unstable. . . . Prison guards exhibit sadistic traits" (p. 453). Furthermore, Haskell and Yablonski cite a Stanford University research experiment conducted in 1971 in which "normal college students . . . demonstrate how the prison environment produces brutality." The prison simulations conducted in the Wheaton College sociology department from 1985 to 1991 clearly demonstrated that college students from good homes with strong Christian values exhibited cruel and sadistic behaviors in a relatively short period of time. These simulations support the Stanford findings.

5. Bud Allen and Diane Bosta, *Games Criminals Play* (Baltimore, MD: American Correctional Institute, 1984, first published by Sacramento, CA: Rae John Publishers, 1981).

Chapter 2: A Place for Healing

1. Many Christians use the Old Testament liberally when talking about the need for severe punishments. In particular, they frequently quote the books of Leviticus and Deuteronomy. However, Pastor Jim Cymbala of the Brooklyn Tabernacle Church, in a personal conversation on 13 October 1991, stated his belief that Christians should not quote the Old Testament without also making reference to the New Testament. According to Cymbala, the old law focuses on strict penalties and retribution while the new law gives more consideration to forgiveness and mercy.

2. Mike McAlari's *Cop Shot* (New York: G.P. Putnam, 1990) contains a description of a defendant being led out of the courtroom: "Cob was swept out of the room like so much garbage, the bounce in his step gone" (p. 279). The reference to "garbage" in this true story is polite considering many common references to criminals by police and prosecutors.

3. David Benner, *Healing Emotional Wounds* (Grand Rapids: Baker, 1990). Dr. Benner, a private clinician and professor at the University of Toronto and McMaster University, was my source for considerable information regarding defense mechanisms to trauma and emotion.

4. Inmate George Del Vecchio, condemned on death row in Menard, Illinois, in the *Daily Illini*, 25 April 1988, in the "perspective section" looks at the system's expression of anger in the form of retaliation and retribution advocating the death penalty as lacking in mercy.

5. In the prologue to his book, *Life Sentence* (Lincoln, VA: Chosen, 1979), Charles Colson speaks of how God used his prison experience to give him the sensitivity to face the struggles and challenges of prison reform and prison ministry.

Chapter 3: The Old Personality in the New Creature

1. This interpretation of 2 Corinthians 5:17, which I support, is also supported by Robert Gromicki, *Stand Firm in the Faith* (Grand Rapids: Baker, 1978), 90–91.

2. See Charles Stanley, *Forgiveness* (Nashville: Oliver Nelson, 1967). Chapter 11 of this book contains a helpful explanation for why people backslide and how we are to restore them within the church. Stanley presents six principles for restoration:

1. Recognize the failure
2. Acknowledge responsibility
3. Confess and repent
4. Restitution
5. Receive God's message
6. Respond to God's chastisement with gratitude

Chapter 4: Who's in Charge?

1. In *The Spark That Ignites* (Minneapolis, MN: Worldwide Publications, 1989), Robert E. Coleman states that "God is always for us. If we who are evil know how

to give good things to our children, how much more will our Father in heaven give the Holy Spirit to them that ask Him (Luke 11:13). Why then should anyone struggle on in spiritual defeat when all the resources of grace are available to the obedient heart?" (p. 37).

2. Robert G. Andry, *Delinquency and Parental Pathology* (London: Staples Press Publishers, 1971),

3. *ABC News*, Evening national news, 4 May 1992.

4. In James Q. Wilson, ed., *Crime and Unemployment: Crime and Public Policy* (San Francisco, CA: Cooper Freeman Publishers and the San Francisco Institute for Contemporary Studies, 1983), Dr. Stevens, professor of Criminal Justice at the University of South Carolina, writes, "The major restraints of crime appear to be centered in individual values such as self-control which are perhaps learned in safe and attentive family environments."

5. In *What Cops Know* (New York: Villard Books, 1991), author Connie Fletcher discusses the subculture of police and the suspicion and mistrust police tend to have for those outside their closed group.

Chapter 5: Hungry for the Spotlight

1. See Judith and Peter M. Blau, "The Cost of Inequality, Metropolitan Structure and Violent Crime," *American Sociological Review*, Fall Edition, 1982. The authors effectively demonstrate that one of the reasons for repeated serious crime and for prisons' failing to deter crimes is that the prison actually fuels anger by being both an "ineffective and exploitative system."

2. In 1989, Zondra Linblade and Dwayne Elmer of Wheaton College completed a survey of American prison ministries commissioned by the Institute for Prison Ministries (Wheaton, IL: Billy Graham Center Publications, 1990). The method of this survey was a random sampling of a comprehensive list of five hundred prison ministries. There was a 71 percent response with a margin of error of plus or minus 3 percent.

Chapter 6: Finding a Church Home

1. This figure was obtained from a cross sampling of prison ministries responding to the above mentioned survey. Prison ministry leader Frank Constantino, said in a speech at Wheaton College in June 1991, that the percentage of unchurched ex-offenders is probably higher.

2. See Donald MacGillis, *Crime in America* (Philadelphia, PA: Radnor Press, 1983), 116. This chapter also gives examples of prisons that have helped inmates develop job skills they can realistically use on the outside.

Chapter 7: The Risk of Loving

1. See Bud Allen and Diana Bosta, *Games Criminals Play* (Santa Ray, CA: Rae John Publishers, 1981), 205, for a concise checklist of victim susceptibility traits.

2. See Tim Cahill, *Buried Dreams* (New York: Bantam, 1986). This book, the story of convicted serial killer John Wayne Gacy, relates Gacy's response to his victim's families: "John prays for them. His message for his victims' families is

'to seek solace in the Bible, in the Word of God above.' Yet John Wayne Gacy is not asking for forgiveness" (p. 371). Although police found the bodies of twenty-nine boys beneath his house, Gacy maintains his innocence—"With God as my witness." This is typical of a sociopath who is able to use religious words as tools of deception.

3. Harry Greene is director of Good News Jail and Prison Ministry in Alexandria, Virginia. This information comes from an interview with Mr. Greene on 24 April 1992 at his ministry offices.

4. For further reading regarding sociopathic personalities see W. McCord and J. McCord, *The Psychopath: An Essay on the Criminal Mind* (New York: Van Nostrand Reinholt, 1964).

5. Psychiatrist C. Markum Berry of Emory University's Department of Psychiatry writes about the sociopathic tendency to prey on church people under the heading "Anti-Social Personality Disorder" in David Brenner, ed., *Baker Encyclopedia of Psychology* (Grand Rapids: Baker, 1985), 64.

6. Recidivism rates related to incarceration for the antisocial personality were studied by Kraft, Stephenson, and Granger, 1964. On national average, 50 percent returned to prison compared to 80 percent of non-antisocial personalities. The implication may be that they evade new arrest because of superior manipulative skills and not rehabilitation.

7. In *Free at Last* (Waco: Word, 1976), Bill Glass states, "One of the most *un-Christian* things anyone can say is 'Those people in prisons are beyond help.' That statement denies the power of Christ to change sinners."

8. Sinclair Lewis, *Elmer Gantry* (New York: NAL Dutton, 1967).

9. Charles Colson, in his book *Kingdoms and Conflicts* (Grand Rapids: Zondervan, 1987), states, "The problem of power is not limited to public officials, of course. It effects all human relationships from the domineering parent, to the bullying boss, to the manipulative spouse, to the pastor who plays God. It is also wielded effectively by the seemingly weak who manipulate others to gain their own ends. The temptation to abuse power confronts everyone, including people in positions of spiritual authority" (p. 271).

Chapter 8: Wise As Serpents

1. For more on restitution see Lois G. Forer, *Criminals and Victims* (New York: W. Norton, 1980). Chapter 18 specifically addresses the need for victim compensation, which encompasses restitution.

2. Dan Van Ness, in Appendix B of his book *Crime and Its Victims* (Downers Grove, IL: InterVarsity, 1986), addresses the issue of "how much restitution" is required. He establishes that punishment should be appropriate to the wrong and that therefore the "eye for an eye" principle is one of limitation, not compulsion. The offender should attempt to restore to the victim what was lost, but without the compounding interest or damages that are often awarded in today's civil courts.

3. The importance of a work ethic for ex-offenders is discussed in Ned Rollo's booklet, *Man, I Need a Job: Finding Employment with a Criminal History* (Dallas: Offender Preparation Education Network, 1991).

Chapter 9: What Can the Church Do?

1. George W. Cornell, "Religion Impacts Prisons," Washington Post, 6 April 1990.

2. It should be noted that African-Americans in the study showed little impact regarding recidivism as a result of religious participation. Burt Rosen, Director of Research for Prison Fellowship, suggested a reason for this in an August 1991 conversation: "In the early years of Prison Fellowship programs, P.F. had not sufficiently developed cross-cultural sensitivity. We can assume future studies will show a greater impact on this segment of the prison population."

3. Reprinted by permission of Hartzel Black of the Correctional Education Division of Southeastern Illinois College. Since 1976, Southeastern Illinois has done innovative work that has gained national attention. Illinois's LEAP program, which began in 1990, provides a good model with obvious implications for the local church.

4. Dr. Tony Campolo, "Sunday's Coming." Address given at the Urbana conference of InterVarsity Christian Fellowship in Champaign, Illinois, 29 December 1989.

5. Ex-offender Richard Coss, in *Wanted* (Gretna, LA: Pelican Publishing Company, 1989) testifies to the importance of a mentoring plan. He claims that Christian role models were a key part of his success after release: "I found that God was continuing to put many fine soul winning Christians in my path so I could continue to grow" (p. 74).

6. These remarks come from a conversation I had with J. Michael Quinlan, director of the Federal Bureau of Prisons, at his Washington D.C., office on 23 April 1992.

7. Another area where older people can be helpful is working as mediators between victims and offenders through Victim Offender Reconciliation Programs. Charles Colson and Dan Van Ness, in their book *Convicted* (Westchester, IL: Crossway, 1989), explain more about how VORP programs can work (p. 85).

8. "Doing Crime: A Survey of California Inmates," a 1980 study by Sampson and Castellano identifies the desire for "high living" (materialism) as the number-one reason for new crime. "Most unemployed individuals who balance the gains of crime versus prison, choose crime."

9. See footnote 6.

10. Prison evangelist Bill Glass states in his book *How to Win When the Roof Caves In* (Old Tappan, NJ: Revell, 1990) that "there is no such thing as cheap victory. It costs a lot of pain and suffering, and you won't find it at the end of a rainbow or at the top of a ladder of success. Victory's price tag reads 'faithfulness, endurance and always sorrow'" (p. 46).

11. Ned Rollo, the Executive Director of Open, Inc., in Dallas, Texas, strongly advocates that ex-offenders take control of their own lives and future. He offers

excellent guidance in the booklets, *Keeping It Together: Social and Psychological Adjustments of Offenders and Their Loved Ones* (Dallas: Offender Preparation Education Network, 1987) and *99 Days and a Get Up: A Manual for Pre and Post Release*, (Dallas: Offender Preparation Education Network, 1988). For information write P.O. Box 566025, Dallas, TX, 75356–6025.

12. John Perkins, in *With Justice for All* (Ventura, CA: Regal, 1982), talks about the need for reconciliation. He is speaking specifically of the Civil Rights struggle, but his words apply to our view of ex-offenders as well: "I didn't yet see them through eyes of compassion. I saw their faults but not their needs. And so my work for justice was motivated by a tempered hostility rather than a love and passion for reconciliation. It is never easy. It requires humbling yourself to say, I'm sorry. It means forgiving. It is a tough, often painful struggle but it is the kind of struggle worth being in" (p. 119).